THE
BEACHES
OF SCOTLAND

THE
BEACHES
OF SCOTLAND

A SELECTED GUIDE TO OVER 150 OF THE MOST BEAUTIFUL
BEACHES ON THE SCOTTISH MAINLAND AND ISLANDS

First published in 2022 by Vertebrate Publishing.

VERTEBRATE PUBLISHING
Omega Court, 352 Cemetery Road, Sheffield S11 8FT, United Kingdom.
www.v-publishing.co.uk

A CIP catalogue record for this book is available from the British Library.

ISBN 978-1-83981-078-7 (Paperback)
ISBN 978-1-83981-079-4 (Ebook)

Front cover: Luskentyre on Harris. © Georgie Gibbon
Back cover: Traigh Shiar, Vatersay; Camusdarach Beach, Lochaber; Singing Sands, Islay;
Inverboyndie Beach © Walkhighlands, Banff; St Ninian's Isle © Walkhighlands, Shetland;
Elgol Beach, Isle of Skye; Sango Bay, the Far North; A' Chlèit, Kintyre.

Photography by Stacey McGowan Holloway unless otherwise credited.

Mapping contains OS data © Crown copyright and database right (2021) and
Openstreetmap.org data © OpenStreetMap contributors.

Cartography by Richard Ross, Active Maps Ltd. *www.activemaps.co.uk*

Design by Jane Beagley, production by Cameron Bonser, Vertebrate Publishing.

Printed and bound in Europe by Latitude Press.

Vertebrate Publishing is committed to printing on paper from sustainable sources.

THE BEACHES OF SCOTLAND

A SELECTED GUIDE TO OVER 150 OF THE MOST BEAUTIFUL
BEACHES ON THE SCOTTISH MAINLAND AND ISLANDS

STACEY McGOWAN HOLLOWAY

Vertebrate Publishing, Sheffield
www.v-publishing.co.uk

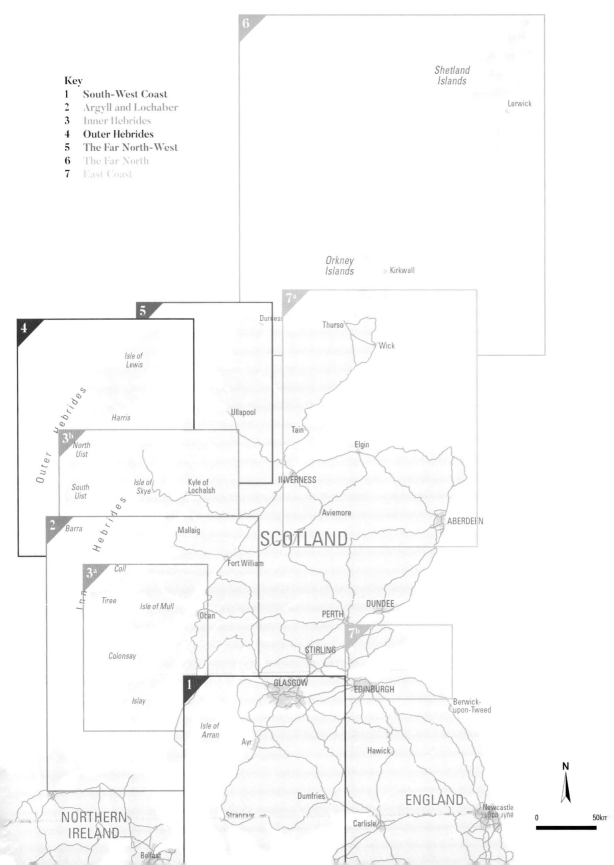

Key
1 **South-West Coast**
2 Argyll and Lochaber
3 Inner Hebrides
4 **Outer Hebrides**
5 The Far North-West
6 The Far North
7 East Coast

Shetland Islands

Lerwick

Orkney Islands   Kirkwall

6

5

4

Isle of Lewis

Outer Hebrides

Harris

Durness   Thurso
Wick

Ullapool

Tain

Elgin

3ᵇ North Uist

South Uist   Isle of Skye   Kyle of Lochalsh

INVERNESS

Aviemore   ABERDEEN

2 Barra

Inner Hebrides

Mallaig

SCOTLAND

Fort William

3ᵃ Coll

Tiree   Isle of Mull

Colonsay   Oban

DUNDEE

PERTH

7ᵇ

STIRLING

Islay

1

GLASGOW   EDINBURGH

Berwick-upon-Tweed

Isle of Arran

Ayr

Hawick

Dumfries   ENGLAND

Stranraer

NORTHERN IRELAND

Carlisle   Newcastle-upon-Tyne

Belfast

N

0   50km

7ᵃ

Opposite David Balfour's Bay, Inner Hebrides

Introduction

When you hear the words 'beach holiday' it automatically conjures up images of lying on golden sands with the sun hot on your skin, relaxing to the sounds of gentle waves and swaying palm trees. Or maybe the quintessential British beach holiday of family-filled shores, ice cream cones and arcade games. However, on Scotland's beaches sunbathing will not be guaranteed!

So, why visit? One of the many answers is that whether they are viewed from the sheltered bulk of a Caledonian MacBrayne (CalMac) ferry as it lumbers out of Ullapool, while glimpsing through a rain-splattered windscreen driving on single-track roads along the Ardnamurchan peninsula or on foot while staring out at the Atlantic Ocean from Balevullin Beach (p63) on Tiree (*Tiriodh*), the coasts of Scotland are powerful and breathtakingly beautiful. When visiting its beaches you are connected to this land in a way that feels both familiar and foreign. There is something almost forgotten about yourself that you are reminded of when you take the effort to reach these remote parts of Britain, these spaces that feel like the edge of the world.

Another reason to visit is that these beaches are truly wild. Whether you want to surf, snorkel, kayak, camp, swim on the open water or just wander peacefully along, these coastlines offer a true escape. Visiting these beaches allows you to have fun, to let your hair fill with salt and your skin be lashed by windblown sand, to enjoy a sunset with family and friends or play in these natural playparks with your children. Here you can forget a world of work and leave responsibilities and worries far behind. Instead, you will be left exhausted and exhilarated, or tranquil and peaceful, in a place where often it is just you, the water and the odd curious seal for a witness.

Acknowledgements

I would like to thank everyone who provided photos of the beaches, local information and knowledge, including Colin S Macleod (*www.hebseaswimmer.com*), Kristin Main, John Phelan, Jennifer Cocking, Georgie Gibbon, Emily Woolard (*www.tartanroad. co.uk*), Eilidh Carr (*www.coralbox.ecwid.com*), Mahalia Scott, Kathie Griffiths, Duncan Griffiths (*www.northuistbunkhouse.co.uk*), Louise Reed, Charlotte Small, Alastair McGowan, Paul Webster (*www.walkhighlands.co.uk*), Douglas Wilcox and Max Holloway. This book could not have become a reality without the detailed editorial work of Jessica McElhattan.

I would also like to thank my family and in particular my husband, Max Holloway, for their never-ending support.

About this book

This book is far from an exhaustive list of Scotland's beaches; it just touches the surface, highlighting the country's finest shores. Some of Scotland's truly hidden gems are not listed here as they can be challenging to reach, and a lot of their magic is in their discovery. The reasons for a beach being chosen for this book were multifactorial, based on its beauty, uniqueness, location and importantly whether it has the infrastructure in place to sustain tourism. Even with this in mind, every location in this book needs to be cared for by those who visit. These are special and beautiful places, which serve as a link to the past through their geology and history, but they are also home to local communities. Many of the facilities located at these beaches are run and funded by these communities or are maintained in partnership between community action groups and local authorities.

In this book you can read about what are often considered as Scotland's most beautiful, fun and interesting beaches. For each beach any available facilities and activities you can undertake there are listed, as well as how to reach the beach. Also included is travel advice to twenty-two of Scotland's islands, including the Isle of Arran, the Isle of Bute, the Inner and Outer Hebrides, the Isle of Skye, Orkney and Shetland.

Top tip
Throughout the book you will find some top tips, which are little insights I have picked up while living in a coastal tourist hotspot and as a tourist myself.

Key

🅿 Parking

🚌 Public transport

🍲 Food and drink

🆆🅲 Toilets

1 Slaggan Bay, the Far North-West
2 Ganavan Sands, Argyll and Lochaber

Beach safety

Within this book there are suggested activities for each beach, including water-based activities such as surfing, kayaking, swimming and stand-up paddleboarding. These are suggestions only and you should only enter the water if you deem it is safe to do so. Weather and tidal conditions can change rapidly and everyone has different abilities. Please read signs on the beaches when you visit about rip tides and undercurrents, and consider the forecast for wind strength and direction if kayaking or stand-up paddleboarding. If you are in any doubt, do not enter the water.

Additionally, seawater temperatures in Scotland are cold all year round, resting between four and sixteen degrees and often below ten degrees. Cold water shock can lead to drowning, so it is not advised to dive or jump straight into the water. Many swimmers and those taking part in water sports in Scotland wear wetsuits all year round.

You may find cows roaming many of the beaches mentioned in this book. If you do, take care not to swim in water contaminated with cow excrement.

In an emergency, call **999** or **112** to contact the emergency services and ask for the coast-guard. Emergency services can also be contacted via SMS text message if you have low phone battery or signal. You must register for this service – to do so send an SMS message, 'register', to 999. EmergencySMS should only be used if a voice call is not possible. Many of the beaches in this book are in remote locations, so ensure you know how to use your phone to determine your exact location.

1 Ardtalla Beach, Inner Hebrides   **2** Talisker Bay, Inner Hebrides

How to visit

Scotland's Right to Roam

The Land Reform (Scotland) Act 2003 gives you a right of responsible, non-motorised access to most of Scotland's unenclosed land and inland water, as well as the foreshore. This means you can cross land and water on foot or by swimming, self-propelled raft (like a paddleboard or kayak), bike or horse, as well as wild camp (this **does not** include camping in vehicles). You can exercise access rights at any time, but you should take special care not to disturb local residents when close to property after dark. Certain situations are not included in these access rights, including the use of a motorised vehicle or vessel (except special vehicles for people with disabilities), accessing land used for field sports or when with a dog or other animal which is not under proper control. There is a right to cross a golf course (excluding golf greens) but not for recreational use of it.

These are your rights **provided you behave sensibly and responsibly**.

Behaving responsibly means acting lawfully and reasonably and not causing unreasonable interference with the rights and interests of others. Three basic principles underpin all this advice:

» Respect the interests of other people.
» Care for the environment.
» Take responsibility for your own actions.

Visit responsibly

Do not litter. This includes dog foul (do not bag it and leave it), toilet paper and sanitary products. Bag everything and carry it out. This book includes where the nearest toilets to a beach, if any, can be found, and in tourist hotspots like the North Coast 500 (NC500) there are free public toilets in many villages. Also note that nearly every ferry port has toilets. If you do need to relieve yourself outside, skip the loo roll or dig a hole and bury the waste far from water sources, paths and buildings.

Do not light fires. These damage the delicate grass areas around the beaches and risk wildfires. If you must have a fire, use a kit that allows burning not to damage the ground and bring your own wood to burn. Do not damage trees, fences or signs, and do not take other people's firewood for your fire.

Close gates and don't damage fences.

Park in dedicated parking spaces. Do not park in passing places, on other people's land, blocking roads including farm access points or on delicate grasslands and machair near beaches.

Follow guidance for wild camping. Wild camping does not include in or next to your vehicle. Wild camping is defined as camping unobtrusively in a remote location, staying for only one or two nights in one location and in a small group. Most importantly, Leave No Trace – if you carry it in, carry it out.

Do not disturb wildlife. This includes using existing paths and wooden walkways in place to protect sand dunes and the delicate grasslands and machair surrounding many Scottish beaches. Increasingly there is a problem of people using stand-up paddleboards or kayaks to approach seals and disturbing them from rocks – DO NOT approach seals or use drones to disturb birds or animals. Keep dogs on the lead around farm animals and in areas with ground-nesting birds. Do not feed animals.

Visit sustainably
Take your litter home. Do not rely on bins in remote places that are sometimes emptied by local people and become easily overfilled.

Leave No Trace. Consider collecting three additional pieces of litter you have found on the beach.

Leave the car behind. Use a bicycle or use public transport and walk to the beach, reducing your carbon footprint and the car burden in these remote places.

Avoid tourist hotspots. Consider visiting in the off season or choosing less tourist-busy locations.

Truly wild camp. Choose remote locations, where no one has noticed your presence. Arrive late and leave early. Leave No Trace, including replacing any rocks you have used by putting them back where you found them.

Stay on campsites. This reduces the impact of 'dirty' camping on the land and in local communities.

Eat and shop local. Seek out local food and produce, which supports local communities.

Volunteer. Take part in beach cleans or help to maintain paths.

Donate. Many of the facilities you use are community-run camping spots and toilets; leaving a monetary donation ensures they can be maintained for future use.

Learn. Research local wildlife and history.

Report. Flag any breaches of access rights. If a path is obstructed by a locked gate or sign, if you are asked to leave an area where you believe that you may have a Right of Access or if you have a query about access rights, contact the local authority. All local authority websites have details on how to report incidences of access rights being obstructed.

Remove All Trace

It is very easy to take a social-media-ready photo on many of the beaches in this book, however there is a real problem of marine litter that cannot be filtered out. On even the most remote beaches there is evidence of litter and fishing waste such as ropes and nets, as well as piles of waste or plastics embedded into the sand and shells. At many of these sites it is difficult to carry this out.

Plastics make up a lot of this litter, which cause harm to not only wildlife but also to human health. When visiting these beaches, challenge yourself and those with you to carry out three extra pieces of litter on top of your own. Many beaches have bins on-site or nearby if you do not wish to dispose of it at home.

Visit the websites below to read more about charities and community groups working to clean up Scotland's beaches, find out more about the impact of marine litter or discover where you can join an organised beach clean.

» Keep Scotland Beautiful – *www.keepscotlandbeautiful.org/ get-involved/volunteer*
» Marine Conservation Society – *www.mcsuk.org/what-you-can-do/ join-a-beach-clean*
» Surfers Against Sewage – *www.sas.org. uk/region/scotland-hebrides*
» Take 3 for the Sea – *www.take3.org*
» Scottish Government – *www.gov.scot/ policies/marine-environment/marine-litter*

Lifeguards

There are only seven lifeguarded beaches in Scotland. Two of these beaches are included in this book, although they are not lifeguarded at all times: Coldingham Sands Beach (p180) and St Andrew's West Sands (p175).

Accessibility on Scotland's beaches

There are unfortunately very few beaches in Scotland that are wheelchair-accessible or have accessible public toilets. There are a few organisations on the east coast that offer beach-adapted wheelchairs for children and adults, such as Beach Wheelchairs in North Berwick and Edinburgh, the Hamish Foundation in St Andrews, Dornoch Beach Wheelchairs in Dornoch and Sea the Change at Coldingham Sands Beach (p180). The latter also has an accessible toilet and accessible parking.

On Tiree you can contact the local ranger to hire beach wheelchairs. Email *ranger@tireetrust. org.uk* or call 07391 239502.

Some beaches in Scotland, albeit very few, have slipways from beachside car parks, such as Ganavan Sands in Oban (p36), or boardwalks along the beach such as on Ayr Beach (p10), Portobello (p176) and Girvan (p8).

More details can be found at:

» *www.beachwheelchairs.org*
» *hamishfoundation.co.uk/beach- wheelchairs*
» *www.visitdornoch.com/enjoy-in-dornoch/ location/dornoch-beach-wheelchairs*
» *www.seathechange.org.uk/coldingham-beach*

Dogs

Please read up-to-date beach information, but in line with Scotland's Right to Roam, dogs are welcome on nearly all of Scotland's beaches if they are under control and dog waste is correctly disposed of. There are some beaches, such as those on the Ayrshire coast, that require dogs to be on a lead at all times during the summer season.

Language

You will notice Scottish Gaelic (Gàidhlig) on signs and in several of the beach names, many of which also have a Norse influence. In this book Gaelic beach names are given where they also have a common or anglicised name, especially in Gaelic-speaking strongholds such as the Outer Hebrides. Some common coastal words to help read the landscape can be found in the Gaelic glossary (p184).

1 Dunnet Bay, the Far North   **2** Coral Beach, Inner Hebrides
3 Litter at Sandwood Bay, the Far North-West

Types of beach

Gravel beaches and spits
Gravel beaches are formed by sediment being carried by rivers on to the coast. Spits are some of Scotland's most dynamic coastal landforms, formed by longshore drift that carries sediment along the beach.

Sandy beaches and sand dunes
Scotland's sand dunes represent seventy-one per cent of the UK's coastal sand resource. Some of our largest beaches are on the Aberdeenshire and Moray coasts and in the Outer Hebrides. Many of the beaches and dunes have formed in the last 4,000 years.

Machair
Machair is a coastal habitat unique to the north-west of Scotland and Ireland which comprises sand with a high shell content, creating fertile land for wild flowers.

Salt marshes
Salt marsh may be found in upper intertidal areas of enclosed shores. Scottish salt marshes make up fifteen per cent of the total UK resource.

The seascape and geology of Scotland's coasts

By Dr Max Holloway, Ocean Physicist at the Scottish Association for Marine Science

The present-day Scottish coastline extends nearly 19,000 kilometres in length, including some 900 islands, of which 93 are inhabited. Most of Scotland's coastline resides in the west; the Highland region alone comprises nearly 5,000 kilometres of coastline including islands (1,900 kilometres excluding islands), followed by Argyll and Bute with nearly 4,000 kilometres. To put this into context, the straight-line distance between the Mull of Kintyre and Cape Wrath is less than 400 kilometres. The west coast is associated with a meandering coastline, coral beaches and machair. The west's twisting coastline provides contrasting conditions of shelter and exposure around every corner – from wave- and storm-enduring rocky headlands abutting the full force of the Atlantic

Ocean to pristine bays of coral sands and turquoise seas that wouldn't look out of place in a Caribbean holiday brochure. In contrast, the east coast is associated with estuaries and long, fine, sandy beaches. These extensive east-coast beaches offer a more depositional and sheltered coastal environment. If you are visiting Scotland, you will rarely be very far from a beach, the furthest point in mainland Scotland from the sea being approximately sixty-five kilometres. A wide variety of coastal environments provides endless opportunities for escape and adventure.

The story behind the formation of Scotland's landscape and coastline is one of ice and fire. Scotland's lands and seas are intimately connected – few places in the world host coastlines that boast such contrast, evident as the coast delves seaward hundreds of metres into sea lochs and ascends landward to 1,000-metre peaks over a horizontal distance of just a few kilometres.

1 Fionnphort Bay, Inner Hebrides   **2** Bay at the Back of the Ocean cave, Inner Hebrides

Scotland's Caledonian mountains were formed around half a billion years ago, during the brief but dramatic Caledonian period, as three continental plates collided (two of which caused the joining of England to Scotland). This crumple zone thrust up mountain chains as high as the Himalaya and fuelled volcanic activity that created the volcanoes underlying Ben Nevis and Glen Coe. Roughly 50 million years ago the Atlantic Ocean opened, separating Scotland from North America and Greenland. This event formed a line of volcanoes running the length of the west coast of Scotland, from St Kilda to Ailsa Craig. Volcanoes remained active for approximately 5 million years, forming Ben More on the Isle of Mull, Ardnamurchan, Rùm, St Kilda, Rockall and, arguably most famously, the Cuillin Hills on Skye.

From around 2.5 million years ago the Quaternary period began, triggering glacial-interglacial cycles of growth and decay of huge northern-hemisphere ice sheets. These ice sheets carved the shapes of Scotland that we see today, grounding down high peaks and cutting away deep glens and deeper fjords which would later be filled with water as the ice sheets melted and sea levels rose. The ice ages helped to emphasise the contrast between Scotland's west and east; glacial erosion was more prominent in the west, while glacial deposition was more common in the east.

During the most recent glaciation, with ice extent peaking between 20,000 and 30,000 years ago, ice covered all of Scotland's mountains and ice streams flowed in the Minch, the Hebrides and the Moray Firth. Most of this ice had retreated by a rapid warming period just under 15,000 years ago. The result of all this geological ebbing and flowing has placed Scotland's landscape at the forefront of geological discovery and created these incredible beaches.

How and when to travel

Weather

Scotland can experience all four seasons in a single day at any time of year. As a rule of thumb, prepare for cold and rain, even in summer. The beauty of Scotland is that it always looks beautiful, so come prepared with waterproof trousers, a coat and a warm layer and enjoy whatever the weather throws at you.

Between late May and late September be aware of midges and clegs (horseflies). Midges are an unfortunate part of Scotland's outdoors, especially in the Highlands and islands. Please also be aware of ticks, which can carry Lyme disease. It is important to remove them correctly (using a tick tool, which can be purchased in most shops in the Highlands) as soon as possible. Please check yourself and your children each evening if you have walked through long grass or undergrowth. If you develop a 'bullseye' reaction at the bite spot after being bitten or experience cold-like symptoms, seek medical advice.

On the north-east coast and Northern Isles in the warmer months of April to September there is a thick sea fog called the haar, which can plummet temperatures and reduce visibility. If visiting in winter, check out the Scottish tradition of entering the Firth of Forth for a 'Loony Dook' on New Year's Day. You will no doubt find others on these popular Scottish beaches to join in with.

A great time of year to travel to Scotland is early spring, between April and May, as the midges have not arrived and the days are longer and tend to be drier. However, it is still cold at this time of year, so come prepared if camping. Do not rule out a winter beach holiday either – not only are there fewer tourists, but also there is something character-building about walking along a cold beach or wild swimming in the sea with snow-capped hills for company. For a truly amazing experience, head to the beaches of the far-north coast, Skye or the Outer Hebrides armed with a blanket and a dram or hot chocolate to witness the Northern Lights on a clear winter night (check out Glendale Skye Aurora Alerts – *www.aurora-alerts.uk*).

Getting there

Ferries – Some of Scotland's finest beaches are located on islands or peninsulas. The ones listed in this book are all accessible via ferry. Most of the islands are serviced by CalMac and nearly all services need to be booked in advance. There are some services that are turn up and go, however it is critical that you check your route for disruption, which occurs regularly. For sailings to Orkney and Shetland bookings need to be made in advance via NorthLink Ferries.

1 Machair   **2** Bay at the Back of the Ocean, *Inner Hebrides*   **3** Halaman Bay, *Outer Hebrides*

Rail links – Make your journey to Scotland a luxury rail adventure by travelling on the Caledonian Sleeper, which leaves London six nights a week. This train services Glasgow and Edinburgh and then splits to stop at Fort William, Inverness and Aberdeen.

There are a few rail routes that can take you from larger cities to the seaside – a perfect way to see more of Scotland's landscape and coastline.

To begin your Scottish adventure, check out these routes:

» Glasgow to Oban
» Glasgow to Morar via Fort William
» Edinburgh to North Berwick and Dunbar
» Aberdeen with a bus service to Fraserburgh
» Inverness to Elgin with a bus service to Lossiemouth
» Inverness to Kyle of Lochalsh with a bus service to Skye
» Inverness to Wick and bus services to Durness
» Inverness with a bus service to Ullapool

Cycling – There are several routes on Sustrans's National Cycle Network (NCN) which span Scotland: please see the Sustrans website for more information (*www.sustrans.org.uk*), as well as various gravel routes. Travelling the Hebridean islands by bike is a fantastic way to explore them, and many islands have bike hire, including ebikes, close to the ferry port, including Gigha, Tiree and Barra. An excellent cycle option for beach visits is the Hebridean Way from Vatersay to the Isle of Lewis.

Bikes can travel at no additional charge on many trains and all CalMac ferries, but it is advised to book bike spots on trains in advance. The Glasgow to Oban train includes a dedicated cycle carriage on selected services. A limited number of bikes can be placed on some of the larger bus routes, however these cannot be booked in advance and are first come, first served. On ferries to Orkney and Shetland bikes must be booked in advance.

Driving – Many of the roads to and around the coast are single-track roads. This requires the use of passing places to allow the flow of traffic in both directions. Look ahead and plan which passing place to use – if the passing place is on the left then pull into it to let the oncoming vehicle pass, and if the passing place is on your right, stop in the road alongside the passing place so the oncoming vehicle can drive into it, allowing for safe passing. You may have to reverse back to a passing place. If you are a slower-moving vehicle, do pull over when safe to allow traffic behind you to overtake safely. Do not park in passing places.

Beware of cyclists, especially near blind corners or summits. Do not attempt to overtake a cyclist on single-track roads – use passing places or wait for the cyclist to be aware of your presence so they can signal you through or move aside.

Note that not all roads are suitable for all vehicles. Two to look out for in particular are the infamous Bealach na Ba road to the Applecross peninsula and the coastal back road from Achnahaird Bay (p128) to Lochinver (en route to Achmelvich Beach – p131) – neither are suitable for motorhomes or caravans. Some roads will be shut in ice, snow or heavy rain, such as the road through Glen Coe or the road via the Rest and Be Thankful viewpoint. Keep an eye on up-to-date road and traffic information.

In some locations there are limited fuel stations or electric vehicle charging points so prepare in advance.

In addition, there are very few places in Scotland really set up for motorhomes and caravans, but beaches that do have campsites for motorhome stopovers have been highlighted. For visitors camping in vehicles (or away from the traditional view of wild camping as defined in Scotland's Right to Roam – pxi), please make use of these campsites and motorhome stopovers.

Top tip
Bigger is not always better. If you are attracted to the idea of campervanning around Scotland, a smaller campervan compared to a motorhome, or even a small motorhome, will be easier to travel in. See How and when to travel (pxviii) to read more about driving on single-track roads and parking.

Suggested itineraries

Day tripping from Edinburgh
Weekend or day trip
If visiting Edinburgh for a short break, take the railway or drive out to one of the stunning sandy beaches along this coast, such as Portobello (p176), or even brave the tidal causeway crossing to Cramond Island (p176).

Road trip on Scotland's Route 66
Long weekend to a week
The Kintyre 66 is a driving route, launched in 2021, which takes in many of the beaches of Kintyre, from sheltered east-coast beaches and their castles to the surf favourites of Machrihanish and Westport Beach (p32). While you're making your way round, why not leave the car at the Tayinloan ferry port and hop over to Gigha for a couple of hours? Here you can collect a rental bike and cycle the six kilometres to the beautiful, clear waters of the Twin Beaches (p35).

Cycle the Hebridean Way
A week
The Hebridean Way is the best way to visit the Outer Hebrides by bike; take a week's holiday and cycle from Barra to either Tarbert on Harris or Stornoway on Lewis, making sure you hit all the beaches on the way, including Barra Sands (p96) and Bagh A'Deas (p92).

North-east adventure
One to two weeks
For something different when it comes to a road trip, consider taking a circular route from Aberdeen and back via Shetland and Orkney, where you can visit Cata Sand (p152) and St Ninian's Isle (p152), and then driving down the east coast from Scrabster, taking in beaches such as Shandwick Bay (p162) and Cullen (p171).

Rail, sail and cycle
One to two weeks
For a longer adventure, take the train from Glasgow to Ardrossan and then sail to Brodick on Arran. Cycle to the ferry port at Lochranza either via Sannox (p15) or by circumnavigating the island to visit Lamlash (p13) and Pirnmill (p14). From Lochranza you can sail to Kintyre on a turn-up-and-go ferry, allowing you to cycle across Kintyre to Kennacraig. From Kennacraig, you can sail to either Port Askaig or Port Ellen on Islay, a charming island with whisky distilleries to explore. To visit more of Scotland's islands you can sail from Port Askaig to Colonsay, and from here you can set off on two wheels again to reach Kiloran Bay (p60).

Alternatively, head to Oban either by train or ferry and cycle to Ganavan Sands (p36). Finally, you can return to Glasgow, exhausted and exhilarated, by the railway.

Easy to reach and even easier to explore, the south-west coast of Scotland is within a short drive of the Borders to the south and Glasgow to the north, and even by public transport you can be on the beach of a remote island within a few hours. The 320 kilometres of stunning coastline in the south-west are the beaches of this author's childhood, and comprise seaside towns, kilometres of sandy shores and island life. In addition, if you're looking for a beach road trip, the South West Coastal 300 route is a perfect choice.

The beaches along the south-west coast are much more urban than many others in Scotland, and as such the water quality is not rated as highly as in the north and far west. However, many of the waters along these beaches are monitored by the Scottish Environment Protection Agency (SEPA), and the more popular beaches are provided with a daily water quality rating, meaning they are still of a good water quality for bathing and swimming.

SOUTH-WEST COAST

Opposite Maidens **Overleaf** Brodick © Walkhighlands

1 Irvine

Dumfries and Galloway

Do not be tempted to overlook the Scottish Lowlands – those who do will miss a beautiful part of the country. Here you will find an undulating coastline of rocky shorelines and sandy beaches, designated Special Areas of Conservation and protected nature reserves. This area is particularly attractive to cyclists, with forest mountain bike trails, great gravel bike routes or planned cycle tours along the South West Coastal 300 all available to take in the beaches. Water sport enthusiasts will not be short of places to sail, kayak and windsurf.

How to visit

BY LAND There are good road links from the Borders and from Glasgow on the A74(M) and M74. If travelling by bike, there are plenty of cycle tour operators in this area, or it is a great place to check out some coastal woodland bike tracks.

There are direct trains from Glasgow to Stranraer. Services from Carlisle to Dumfries also run.

BY SEA There is a direct ferry from Belfast to Cairnryan, just north of Stranraer.

Rockcliffe

REGION   **Dumfries and Galloway**   LAT/LONG **54.868, -3.807**   GRID REF **NX 848535**   BEACH FACES **South-west**
ACTIVITIES **Walking, spotting the wildlife, exploring the nature reserve, visiting Rough Island**

Often described as one of Scotland's most beautiful coastlines, Rockcliffe's beach is based along the Solway Firth and part of a National Scenic Area and is a National Trust for Scotland nature reserve. Take a meander along the three-kilometre stretch of beach and coastal trails between Kippford and Rockcliffe to see wild flowers, woodlands and meadows. It is best to visit on a low tide, where the shallow beach stretches out almost a kilometre and a half.

Lying just off the coast, there is a bird sanctuary on Rough Island that can be reached on foot at low tide, except during May and June when the birds own the island.

Access

Rockcliffe is signposted off the A710. There is a car park and public toilets in the village.

Luce Sands

REGION   **Stranraer**   LAT/LONG **54.815, -4.953** GRID REF **NX 113523**   BEACH FACES **South-east**
ACTIVITIES **Surfing, windsurfing, kitesurfing**

Luce Sands, also known as Sandhead, is thought by many to be the finest beach in the Stranraer area, and it is designated as a Special Area of Conservation (SAC) due to its dune, seashore and seabed habitats. The beach is ten kilometres long, and at low tide it can extend far out into the bay. The bay is also very popular with surfers and windsurfers and is claimed to be the ultimate kitesurfing location on the south-west coast: the shallow, warm waters and abundance of space make it a great location for beginners.

Access

Beach access is from the Sand of Luce Holiday Park campsite.

1

2

Ayrshire

These west-facing beaches along the south-west mainland coast are the places to go for spectacular sunsets, long expanses of sand, wild swimming, family days out and stunning walks. Many lie close to townships and all are within easy access of Glasgow, meaning these beaches allow day trips away from busy life, and fleeting escapes from the city.

Ayrshire is a great location for culture, seafood and sailing, and is the birthplace of Scotland's National Bard, Robert Burns. Why not have a winter beach break and visit in January to celebrate Burns Night?

How to visit

BY LAND There are good road links from the Borders up the coast to Largs, along the A76 and A78. There are direct trains from Glasgow to and from Irvine, Ayr and Largs.

BY SEA There are ferry links from Dunoon to Gourock and Wemyss Bay to Rothesay.

Girvan

REGION **Ayrshire**   LAT/LONG **55.242, -4.862**
GRID REF **NX 180980**   BEACH FACES **West**
ACTIVITIES **Bathing, walking, taking a dip in the pool, running around a playpark**

Girvan is one of Ayrshire's most popular beaches, and the eponymous town offers a variety of traditional seaside activities, including an amusement centre and fish and chip shop just behind the beach. Like many on Ayrshire's coast, this beach is a wide, long, sandy arc, and the area is part of the UNESCO Biosphere in recognition of its abundance of wildlife and the landscape. Towards the north end of the beach is a small harbour and pier, and there is also a bench-lined promenade, playpark and outdoor paddling pool.

The spectacular island of Ailsa Craig, which is now a bird reserve, lies opposite the beach. The island's unique granite means that it is perfect for making curling stones; nearly all of the curling stones for the Winter Olympics and Winter Paralympics are from Ailsa Craig.

Access

Girvan railway station is just under half a kilometre from the beach, which offers direct rail services to Glasgow. There is a large car park at the harbour with public toilets.

Turnberry

REGION **Ayrshire**   LAT/LONG **55.309, -4.838**
GRID REF **NS 198055**   BEACH FACES **West**
ACTIVITIES **Walking, golfing**

Turnberry's wide, sandy beach is backed by the famous Ailsa course at Trump Turnberry luxury hotel, a regular course on the Open Championships. It is worth walking up to see Trump Turnberry Luxury Collection Resort (as in Donald Trump), which is a stunning building. To the north of the beach it is possible to walk to Turnberry Lighthouse, which is now converted into a suite of the Trump Turnberry. The lighthouse is built on the site of Turnberry Castle, the alleged birthplace of Robert the Bruce.

While being an excellent place for golfers, this area is also very popular for walkers, with the Ayrshire Coastal Path passing the beach.

Access

Parking can be found on the A719 in the village of Turnberry, close to the beach.

1 Girvan **2** Turnberry © Shutterstock/scruffylookingnerfherder **3** Maidens

Maidens

REGION **Ayrshire** LAT/LONG **55.335, -4.816**
GRID REF **NS 214083** BEACH FACES **North-west**
ACTIVITIES **Walking, discovering Ayrshire's history**

Maidens is a quiet and peaceful beach, with a harbour to the south end which has small sea stacks leading out into the ocean.

The beach is a mix of sand and rocks and a popular spot for walking, especially as the start point to walk round the grounds of Culzean Castle and country park – there is even a beach within the grounds named after the castle. You may need to purchase a ticket to enter the gardens and castle.

Access

Bus services to the town of Maidens run regularly from Ayr. There is a car park off Harbour Road at the southern end of the beach, with public toilets nearby.

Ayr Beach

REGION **Ayrshire**   LAT/LONG **55.458, -4.642**
GRID REF **NS 330220**   BEACH FACES **West**
ACTIVITIES **Bathing, cycling, enjoying a picnic, enjoying the putting green or crazy golf**

Located in the bustling town of Ayr, this mostly sandy beach stretches several kilometres and has beautiful views over Arran. The beach, which was bestowed with a Seaside Award from Keep Scotland Beautiful, is lined by a kilometre-and-a-half-long promenade which offers plenty to do, including gardens, a children's playpark and a boardwalk. Also on the seafront is Pirate Pete's Family Entertainment Centre with indoor soft play, mini golf and laser games. Alternatively, the Ayr seafront is part of Sustrans' NCN Route 7, and is a great location to cycle.

Access
The beach is signposted from Ayr town, where you will find good public transport links via Ayr railway station and Ayr bus station. There is street-side parking and a large car park along the beachfront.

Troon Beach

REGION **Ayrshire**   LAT/LONG **55.541, -4.662**
GRID REF **NS 320306**   BEACH FACES **South-west**
ACTIVITIES **Bathing, walking, cycling, enjoying a picnic, golfing**

With an esplanade at its northern end and views across to Arran, it isn't difficult to see why this popular, sandy beach won a Scotland's Beach Award in 2021 from Keep Scotland Beautiful. Troon Beach has that bucket-and-spade, family beach feel to it, however the beach is wilder to the south where it backs on to the dunes of the Royal Troon Golf Club. The water is shallow and great for a paddle, and along the back of the beach are paths for both cycling and walking.

Access
Troon railway station is 500 metres away. There is a car park with public toilets at the north end of the beach; the car park will fill up quickly.

Irvine

REGION **Ayrshire**   LAT/LONG **55.604, -4.694**
GRID REF **NS 304376**   BEACH FACES **South-west**
ACTIVITIES **Swimming, walking, enjoying a picnic, running round a playpark**

Irvine Beach is a beautiful, long stretch of sandy beach that reaches from Saltcoats in the north to Barassie Sands in the south. Irvine Beach is just south of the mouth of the River Irvine, and is very clean, with lots of bins and an electronic sign with daily water quality information for swimmers during the summer. The beach also boasts a lake and huge park behind it, making it a perfect place to come for a walk, a swim in the sea or a day out with the family. However, the beach highlight is the mighty Stone Dragon situated towards the south end of the park. A short walk from the car park, the dragon can be found perched high on the sand dunes overlooking the sea, and is said to be guarding the coastline from future Viking invasions – perfect for children to clamber over.

Access
Irvine railway station is a kilometre and a half away. By car, turn off from the A78 to the A71 towards Irvine, then head west through the town until you reach Beach Drive; there is a free car park at end of this road, with public toilets (by donation). From the beach car park there are steps or a slope down to the beach.

1

2

3

Isle of Arran

Arran is a fantastic island to visit and is only a short ferry ride from the mainland. Known as 'Scotland in miniature', a visit to Arran allows you to enjoy a true Scottish experience in a small-island package. As well as fantastic road cycling, spectacular rock climbing and exhilarating hillwalking, the island also boasts several castles, gardens, local produce, distilleries and an abundance of wildlife. On top of all this, you are treated to a good selection of beaches and water-based activities, ranging from town-side bays on the west coast, which are perfect for ice cream and sandcastle building, to long stretches of white sands on the east with views out to Kintyre, Jura and the wide Atlantic Ocean. These beaches give you that feeling of getting away from it all, and throughout your visit the unique Arran skyline offers a stunning backdrop. Here you will even find a gin bar serving local gins on the beach!

How to visit

BY LAND The island is geared up for cycle tourers and there are good bus links available, with regular services between Brodick and Sannox.

BY SEA To reach Arran you can sail to Brodick from Ardrossan, which has a rail connection from Glasgow. If travelling from Kintyre there is a sailing to Brodick from Campbeltown. Alternatively, ferries run from Clanoig to Lochranza in the north of Arran – in summer this service sometimes departs from Tarbert, so check the timetables closely.

> **Top tip**
> Why not take the bus to Sannox (p15) and hike back over Goat Fell, the island's highest peak, via the airy ridgelines above Glen Sannox?

Brodick and Lamlash

REGION **Arran**
BRODICK
LAT/LONG **55.587, -5.154**   GRID REF **NS 013371**
BEACH FACES **East**
....
LAMLASH
LAT/LONG **55.531, -5.128**   GRID REF **NS 026307**
BEACH FACES **East**
....
ACTIVITIES **Bathing, walking, running around a playpark, enjoying a tipple at the gin bar, exploring the local towns**

Brodick and Lamlash are two wide, east-facing bays. Although not always the most picturesque beaches both are very convenient, especially for families, and when the sun is shining they can be glorious. Both are located at the edge of busy towns, meaning they are near a lot of hotels and bed and breakfasts, with large greens, playparks and shops metres from the beach – perfect for a day out with the family. To the far north end of Brodick, near to the castle, you will even find a gin bar on the beach, where you can sample gin made on the island and book tasting sessions.

Lamlash is a quieter village which provides a stunning view out to Holy Island on a sunny day. Holy Island is home to a Buddhist Centre for World Peace and Health, after the Virgin Mary reputedly persuaded the previous owner to sell the island in a dream. The rest of the island is a nature reserve. If you take a boat and visit the island, be sure to drink from the supposedly healing spring.

Access

Brodick is served by ferries from Ardrossan harbour in Ayrshire. Public car parks are available at both beaches with direct access to the beach.

Blackwaterfoot

REGION **Arran**   LAT/LONG **55.504, -5.340**
GRID REF **NR 891284**   BEACH FACES **South-east**
ACTIVITIES **Walking, spotting the wildlife, discovering Arran's history, golfing**

A large, long beach of sand and rocks, situated next to the small village of Blackwaterfoot. From the beach there is a coastal walk which passes the impressive Drumadoon Point, a breeding area for fulmar, jackdaw and kestrel. Divers and black guillemot can also be seen here.

Further along the coastal path you come to King's Cave. It is claimed that Robert the Bruce hid in this cave after his disastrous first year as King of Scots. Legend says that while waiting out the winter of 1306, he watched a spider on the cave wall. Bruce took inspiration from the spider never giving up on spinning its web, and resolved to continue his campaign against the English. However, ancient carvings and Pictish symbols found on the walls suggest that Bruce wasn't the cave's first inhabitant. Using paths through the forestry, this can be made into a circular walk back to the beach.

Access

Regular buses stop at Blackwaterfoot from Brodick. This is a very accessible beach, with a small car park on the waterfront opposite the golf course.

Pirnmill

REGION **Arran**   LAT/LONG **55.643, -5.383**
GRID REF **NR 871439**   BEACH FACES **West**
ACTIVITIES **Paddling, walking**

A long stretch of picturesque coastline along Arran's north-west coast, Pirnmill's beach is a thin strip of pure-white sand and clear,

blue waters. There are several villages along this coast, including Catacol and Pirnmill.

Be aware that this coast often sees lion's mane jellyfish in the summer months, which can leave a nasty sting. You will often see them washed up along the beach.

Access

Regular buses stop at Pirnmill from Brodick and Blackwaterfoot. The A841 runs alongside the beach; there is very limited roadside parking.

Sannox

REGION **Arran** LAT/LONG **55.662, -5.153**
GRID REF **NS 017454** BEACH FACES **East**
ACTIVITIES **Bathing, hiking, walking, spotting the wildlife**

A family-friendly beach, with pretty, white sand mixed with colourful, smooth pebbles. Views to the east are across the water towards mainland Scotland, but to the west the beach is overlooked by the domineering mountains of Glen Sannox and the corrie of the Devil's Punchbowl. The name Sannox comes from the Viking *sand-vik*, meaning sandy bay.

Starting from the beach is the Fallen Rocks Coastal Trail, a coastal walk taking you past the Fallen Rocks, giant sandstone boulders that fell in a landslide from the cliffs above. It leads you to a picnic site and spot to look for gannets, dolphins, porpoises and basking sharks. Across the road from the beach is also the start of hiking routes through Glen Sannox and, for the experienced hikers, routes up to the dramatic ridges on both sides of the glen.

Access

Regular buses stop at Sannox from Brodick. There is a small car park at Sannox with public toilet. From here, head down the path to the north of the car park where you can cross the river via large stepping stones and follow the path to the beach.

Argyll and Lochaber have everything you could want in a beach destination. Visit this mainland region for mountain vistas, coastal golf resorts and spas, fresh seafood, water-bound castles, wild swimming, wild kayak trails, remote and rugged coastal roads and an abundance of seaside wildlife.

This is a location full of history and an expansive range of mind-blowing landscapes, but without the tail backs of the overly popular North Coast 500 route (and significantly fewer midges). For a thrilling journey, take a road trip from lowlands to the Highlands on the Kintyre 66, on which you can visit beaches full of history and drive along winding coastal roads from Tarbert to the Corran Narrows, visiting Oban and its family-friendly bays. You can then sail across the Corran Narrows or drive the Road to the Isles (*Rathad nan Eilean*) to reach the rugged remoteness of the Ardnamurchan peninsula. Here rests the haven of Sanna Bay (p41), as well as beautiful forests and bare coasts which lead to Singing Sands (p42). After this detour west, head north to Arisaig to be immersed in silver sands and clear waters, rivalled only by those in the Outer Hebrides. Some of Scotland's most beautiful beaches lie along this peninsula, located between Oban and Mallaig.

ARGYLL
AND LOCHABER

Opposite A' Chlèit Beach **Overleaf** Sanna Bay

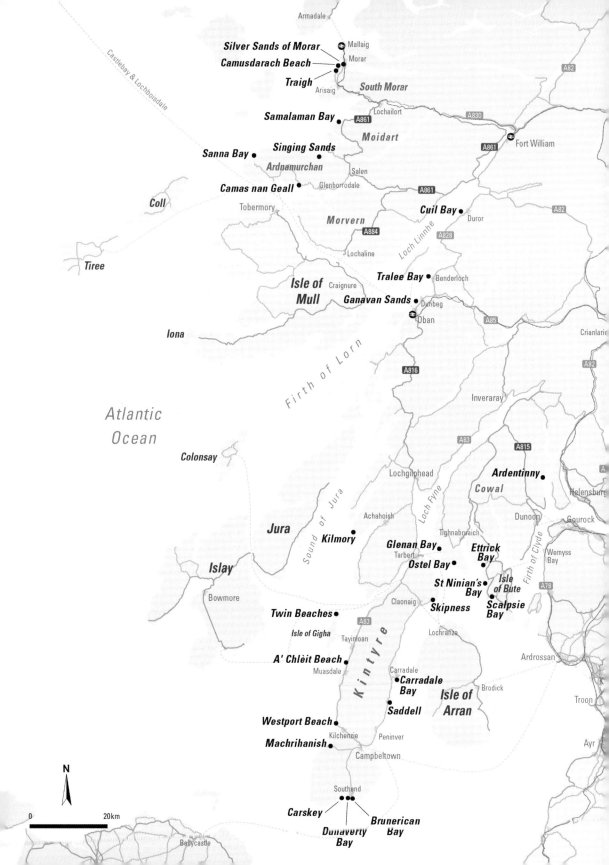

1 Glenan Woods, Glenan Bay

Cowal and Bute

The Cowal peninsula is often referred to as Argyll's Secret Coast: in a relatively short distance you can travel from the bustling outskirts of Glasgow to the remote, frayed edges of mainland Scotland. Surrounded by crofts, complicated coastlines and rollercoaster roads, you will continuously want to pull over to take in the views.

Despite being part of mainland Scotland, Cowal is enclosed by the Firth of Clyde to the east and Loch Fyne on the west, as well as several sea lochs in between, meaning the easiest way to visit may be by boat.

By contrast, the Isle of Bute feels like the mainland despite being an island. However, this feeling dissipates quickly as you travel west away from the bigger towns of Rothesay and Port Bannatyne and into farmland, with views to the west of the Argyll islands and peninsulas beyond. Bute is a very popular place for road cycling, for both visitors and locals, and there are budding community cycling and road cycling clubs on the island. You will also find cycle service

points dotted around. All of this makes Bute a very cycling-friendly island, and just about all of the beaches can be visited by bike.

How to visit

BY LAND From the east and the north of Scotland, following the A83 in a car is possible, but be aware of road closures near the Rest and Be Thankful viewpoint. Trains from Glasgow to Gourock allow you to then catch the ferry to Dunoon.

BY SEA Ferry sailings that accommodate cars can be made from Gourock to Dunoon and from Tarbert in Kintyre to Portavadie. There are also boat and rail options for passengers both on foot and bike to travel from Glasgow to Dunoon. To reach Bute, there are two Cal-Mac ferry services, either from Wemyss Bay to Rothesay or Colintraive in Cowal to Rhubodach. These are turn-up-and-go ferries with no need to book, and have regular sailings.

Scalpsie Bay

REGION **Bute**   LAT/LONG **55.779, -5.098**
GRID REF **NS 057584**   BEACH FACES **South-west**
ACTIVITIES **Swimming, walking, stand-up paddle-boarding, kayaking**

Although Scalpsie Bay was once used by the military during the Second World War, now this picturesque, crescent-moon-shaped beach provides a family-friendly location that is great for swimming, kayaking and stand-up paddleboarding. The beach feels like a bolthole away from Glasgow despite its relative accessibility, and with the surrounding farmland it is an idyllic getaway location. There are several waymarked walking trails located in the wooded areas and higher land to the north of the beach, accompanied by boards with maps of the walks and information on local history.

The highlights of this bay are the views of Arran, the Holy Isle and the 200-strong local seal colony. One of the viewpoints, Seal View, allows you to see the seals basking on the rocks, and another viewpoint lies higher up near the road.

Access
The nearest bus service stops in Stravanan from Ettrick Bay (p25), and from here it is a five-kilometre walk to the beach. There is a small car park to the west of the beach, with a viewing platform and a map, where you can see across to Arran; short trails lead down to the beach and nearby locations of interest. If taking the steep trail down to the beach from the viewing platform be aware of cows in the field. Further along the main road there is another small car park at sea level.

St Ninian's Bay

REGION **Bute**   LAT/LONG **55.809, -5.128**
GRID REF **NS 040618**   BEACH FACES **South**
ACTIVITIES **Bathing on a high tide, walking, kayaking, discovering Bute's history**

St Ninian's Bay is a kilometre-long horseshoe beach and natural anchorage comprised of a mix of sand, cockleshell and rocks, all protected by a spit of land called St Ninian's Point. The bay is also home to St Ninian's Chapel, an early Christian site, although the chapel's location means it is cut off from the mainland at high spring tides and during storms. The beach has a signposted trail around its perimeter, allowing access to the chapel ruins. You can also seek out the two small standing stones at the north-eastern edge of St Ninian's Bay, immediately beside the path.

This is a peaceful place to visit and to take a walk, and from the beach you get fabulous views of Inchmarnock, the four-kilometre-long satellite isle to the west of Bute. North of the beach and trail is farmland and a large swathe of salt marsh.

Access
From the A844 take the turning to Straad at The Pencil Box, a phone-box honesty gift shop. Take the track heading right around the houses which leads to a small parking area by the beach.

Ettrick Bay

REGION **Bute** LAT/LONG **55.850, -5.140**
GRID REF **NS 036663** BEACH FACES **South-west**
ACTIVITIES **Swimming, walking, cycling, stand-up paddleboarding**

Ettrick Bay is a long, crescent-moon-shaped beach and one of the most popular on Bute. There is access at both ends of the beach and a sandy path from one end to the other that makes a pleasant walk or cycle, although take care as there are some very sandy sections. This is a beach where it is best to visit at mid-tide, as most of the sand is covered by the sea at high tide. A great spot for a family day out, the very shallow water reaching far out into sea makes this a lovely location for children to play. When you've finished exploring, at the northern end of the beach there is the often busy but very friendly Ettrick Bay Tea Room, with covered outdoor seating.

Access

There are car parks at both ends of the beach; a cafe, bike lock stand and bus stop (with regular buses to Rothesay) are at the north end of the beach.

Ardentinny

REGION **Cowal** LAT/LONG **56.055, -4.907**
GRID REF **NS 191885** BEACH FACES **South-east**
ACTIVITIES **Paddling, walking, cycling, enjoying a picnic or barbecue, campervanning, spotting the wildlife**

Ardentinny's beach is on the sea loch of Loch Long. Set in a woodland, it has a different atmosphere and landscape to many other beaches. This is a perfect family picnic spot with benches under the trees overlooking the sandy and shelled beach. The picnic tables even have barbecue rests built into them, so as to avoid damaging the benches. While you enjoy your picnic, keep an eye out for red squirrels.

Various woodland walking trails pass here, with some suitable for wheelchairs and buggies, and for further exploration Glenfinart Walled Garden is nearby. Beside the beach are also overnight hardstanding spots for campervans (free, but you will need your own toilet onboard).

There is quite a history of military use in Loch Long and at Ardentinny's beach. During the Second World War, Royal Navy beach commandos trained for the Normandy landings here, and between 1912 and 1986 the loch was used as a torpedo firing range. Even today, military submarines can sometimes be seen in the loch.

Access

Local buses run from Dunoon to Ardentinny village. By car, head north from Ardentinny village. There is a turning on the right just beyond the entrance to Glenfinart Caravan Park – follow this path and go over a small bridge on the left. The car park is just beyond the bridge. You can also access the beach from the north end of the village. There are public toilets on the picnic site.

Ostel Bay

REGION **Cowal**   LAT/LONG **55.852, -5.262**
GRID REF **NR 959669**   BEACH FACES **South**
ACTIVITIES **Bathing, walking, exploring the nature reserve**

Ostel Bay is a special beach, which can only be reached on foot via a kilometre-and-a-half walk through a nature reserve along a path starting near Kilbride Farm. Be aware your feet may get wet as the ground can be boggy on the way. What makes this beach unique are the views across the water to Arran and its remote location. Although you should not expect the aquamarine waters of the Kintyre coast or Hebridean beaches, this is still a stunning beach fringed with marram grass and golden sands.

There is also a weather-dependent cafe, The Bothy, at Kilbride Farm, where you can get snacks and drinks.

Access
The single-track roads on this remote peninsula of Cowal are accompanied by stunning scenery. From Kilbride Farm follow the path through the nature reserve for approximately a kilometre and a half on foot to the beach. Do not follow the satnav route, as there is no access via the private road; very limited parking in a lay-by near Kilbride Farm.

Glenan Bay

REGION **Cowal**   LAT/LONG **55.881, -5.323**
GRID REF **NR 921705**   BEACH FACES **West**
ACTIVITIES **Swimming, walking, relaxing at a spa**

This is a rugged beach in Glenan Bay, which can easily be visited from Portavadie ferry port via either the coastal or woodland paths through Glenan Woods. These routes are waymarked and have a colour-coded map as you enter the woods. The walks can be done as a looped route. It is approximately two kilometres to the beaches, which can be taken in as part of a looped walk, and you will need sturdy shoes, especially if it is wet underfoot. However, the coastal walk to the pebbled beaches is well worth it, taking you through what feels like an ancient fairy tale footpath, guarded by gnarled trees growing among the quartz and schist rocks. If you carry on further, you will eventually reach a sandy beach and a wild swim spot.

If Scottish wild swimming is not for you, why not visit the nearby Lodge spa at Portavadie Marina hotel, with its outdoor infinity pool overlooking the loch?

If you want to explore further, Portavadie also happens to be the start of the ninety-two-kilometre Cowal Way long-distance walking route.

Access
There is a car park with public toilets at the Portavadie ferry port, where buses from Dunoon also stop. From the Portavadie ferry car park, follow the coastal or woodland paths through Glenan Woods.

Kintyre

Scotland's most southerly peninsula is often referred to as a 'mainland island' due to its remoteness. A highlight of Kintyre is that this remote, rural location is very accessible and free from the usual tourist crowds. The place that inspired Sir Paul McCartney to write 'Mull of Kintyre' is still one of Scotland's best-kept secrets, with its views of islands on either side, including the impressive silhouette of Arran on the east, as well as rolling hills, amazing driving and stunning beaches. The Kintyre 66 route offers a chilled-out, 106-kilometre (or 66-mile) road trip, with all the beaches on the way easily accessible.

In addition, be sure to hop over to the Isle of Gigha – this is one island and beach not to miss.

How to visit

BY LAND The road from Oban to Campbeltown is a fantastic drive, but the section between Oban and Lochgilphead includes a section with multiple tight hairpins. It is very easy to drive around Kintyre, but be aware the route along the east coast is single-track in places. Kintyre is difficult to travel around via public transport: there are no railway stations in the peninsula, but local buses run throughout.

BY SEA If travelling from Cowal there are ferry sailings from Portavadie to Tarbert. From Arran there are ferries from Lochranza to Claonaig (check the timetable for this ferry as sometimes it sails to and from Tarbert). You can also reach Kintyre from Northern Ireland if you sail on a passenger-only ferry: this service links Campbeltown in Kintyre and Ballycastle on the Antrim Coast.

Skipness

REGION **East Kintyre**   LAT/LONG **55.766, -5.337**
GRID REF **NR 905576**   BEACH FACES **South**
ACTIVITIES **Walking, discovering Kintyre's history, sampling some seafood**

Skipness is a pebble-and-shingle beach over-looked by the airy ridges of Arran. This is a quiet and tranquil shore, with a castle and chapel on the banks to visit (free admission to the grounds). Complete a perfect day here with fresh and sustainably sourced local seafood from the seasonal Skipness Seafood Cabin, located at Skipness Castle.

Access

There are two access points to the beach either side of the river mouth. The first is as you enter the village of Skipness. Carry on along the road through the village and there is a car park close to the castle, where infrequent buses from Lochgilphead also stop. Take the path past the castle and through the sheep field to reach the beach.

Carradale Bay

REGION **East Kintyre**   LAT/LONG **55.581, -5.470**
GRID REF **NR 811374**   BEACH FACES **South**
ACTIVITIES **Swimming, walking, stand-up paddleboarding, spotting the wildlife, discovering Kintyre's history**

Carradale Bay is a real gem of a beach and the one you should make sure to visit on the east Kintyre coast. A long, wide stretch of golden sand with sheltered, shallow crystal-clear water makes a tranquil and peaceful location that is perfect for wild swimmers or for taking a stroll along the sand.

On the east side of the beach is Carradale Point, where the Scottish Wildlife Trust has a nature reserve with feral goats. A 2,000-year-old fort is also located on a small tidal island off Carradale Point headland.

Access

Sandy car park at the beach, or parking available in the village just under a kilometre away, where buses from Campbeltown stop. There is also a shop in the village.

Saddell

REGION **East Kintyre**   LAT/LONG **55.528, -5.501**
GRID REF **NR 793317**   BEACH FACES **South**
ACTIVITIES **Swimming, exploring the castle**

Like Carradale Bay, Saddell is a south-facing, sheltered bay with a wide swathe of golden sands. The sixteenth-century tower of Saddell Castle is located right on the waterfront, looking out across the Kilbrannan Sound to Arran; you can treat yourself to a stay in the castle. Here you will also find one of five Antony Gormley sculptures commissioned by the Landmark Trust. This life-size iron figure is the only one in Scotland. If the beach looks familiar, it may be because it was where the video for Sir Paul McCartney's 'Mull of Kintyre' was filmed.

Access

Just under a kilometre from Saddell village, where there is a small car park and infrequent buses to Campbeltown and Carradale.

Brunerican Bay and Dunaverty Bay

REGION **Mull of Kintyre**
BRUNERICAN BAY: LAT/LONG **55.309, -5.639** GRID REF **NR 691076** BEACH FACES **South**

DUNAVERTY BAY: LAT/LONG **55.309, -5.645** GRID REF **NR 688077** BEACH FACES **South**

ACTIVITIES **Swimming, walking, golfing**

Brunerican Bay and Dunaverty Bay are two south-facing beaches located near the village of Southend. As the village name suggests, these beaches are located on the most southerly point of the Mull of Kintyre, facing towards the nineteen-kilometre stretch of sea between Scotland and Northern Ireland.

Both beaches have a mix of sand and pebbles. Brunerican hugs the coast beside the golf course, whereas Dunaverty stretches from the road just beyond Southend to the former lifeboat station below Dunaverty Rock. The highlight of these beaches is the walk between them, which allows you to visit both Dunaverty Rock and the Roaring Cove: Dunaverty Rock is an imposing rock standing at the same elevated height, and just metres away from, the abrupt headland, with steep drops into the sea; the Roaring Cove was created by waves being forced into the crevasse in the headland.

Access

These beaches are located on the south coast of the Mull of Kintyre. There is parking nearby (with public toilets) at Dunaverty Bay on the B842. Access to Brunerican Bay is through the golf course. Muneroy Stores & Tea Room is a kilometre from the beaches.

Carskey

REGION **Mull of Kintyre** LAT/LONG **55.308, -5.672** GRID REF **NR 669077** BEACH FACES **South**
ACTIVITIES **Bathing, walking, discovering Mull of Kintyre's history**

Carskey is an idyllic, sandy beach backed by dunes situated on the Mull of Kintyre, where St Columba, an Irish abbot, supposedly first stepped foot on the Scottish mainland. From the beach car park follow the trail alongside the road to reach some footprints carved into the rock, allegedly St Columba's, and a holy well. Footprints carved into stones are found in a number of places in Ireland and Scotland, and are usually associated with king-making ceremonies. Further along visit the Keil Caves.

Access

There is a car park directly across the road from the beach. Buses to Campbeltown can be caught just under a kilometre further west along the B842.

1

2

3

31

Machrihanish and Westport

REGION **West Kintyre**
WESTPORT: LAT/LONG **55.474, -5.712**   GRID REF **NR 655261**   BEACH FACES **West**

MACHRIHANISH: LAT/LONG **55.424, -5.730**   GRID REF **NR 640208**   BEACH FACES **West**

ACTIVITIES **Walking, surfing, golfing**

Machrihanish is a five-kilometre-long beach which lies on the Mull of Kintyre peninsula, between the small village of Machrihanish to the south and Westport Beach to the north. Backing both Machrihanish and Westport beaches is Argyll's largest mainland dune system, a Site of Special Scientific Interest for its wild flowers, butterflies and moths.

Both beaches are popular with surfers, in particular the Westport end. However, there are strong currents and rip tides here, so both beaches are not suitable for swimming or paddling. Nonetheless, Machrihanish Beach is backed by a golf course, and further south along the coast rests a seabird and wildlife sanctuary, making these beaches perfect for long walks.

Access
Buses to Campbeltown can be caught on the B843 through Machrihanish. Parking at the Machrihanish end of the beach just past the golf course; there are also public toilets here. There is a large car park at Westport end with information on the rips and currents.

A' Chlèit Beach

REGION **West Kintyre**   LAT/LONG **55.614, -5.684**   GRID REF **NR 681418**   BEACH FACES **West**
ACTIVITIES **Bathing, walking**

A' Chlèit Beach is a thin strip of white sand and rocks. From the eighteenth-century A' Chlèit Church there are steps and an inviting wooden jetty, funded by several local community groups and businesses, that leads to the beach. A sign on the walkway informs you that A' Chlèit is Gaelic for promontory (or point) and pronounced 'klaych'; it is a word also linked to the Norse word *klettr*, for rocks or cliff.

Directly behind A' Chlèit Church there are beautiful views out to Jura. With its little sheltered swim spot just further along the back of the church, this is a wonderful beach to take a sunset walk or little sea dip, and a favourite with local people.

Access
Turn off the A83 just north of Muasdale Holiday Park taking the short road to A' Chlèit Church. There is a small car park and wooden walkway and steps leading to the beach.

Twin Beaches

REGION **Isle of Gigha, Kintyre**
LAT/LONG **55.723, -5.734**   GRID REF **NR 655540**
BEACH FACES **North and south**   ACTIVITIES **Swimming, cycling, stand-up paddleboarding**

Travel to the small island of Gigha just off the west coast of Kintyre and discover a mini oasis. The Twin Beaches are linked by a tombolo, so you have a choice of facing either north or south. The north beach is a stunning open water swim spot, with clear waters and white sands dotted with white and silver shells.

The Isle of Gigha is the location of Wee Isle Dairy, a family-owned business producing milk and artisan ice cream. Be sure to sample their produce while visiting Argyll and Bute; most local and community-run shops stock it and you can return glass bottles to the shop for the dairy to collect and re-use. After your visit to the Twin Beaches, be sure to visit the Achamore Gardens and local restaurant The Boathouse.

Access
Catch the CalMac ferry to Gigha from Tayinloan on the west coast of Kintyre. This service docks near Ardminish. There are public toilets at the ferry port. Although you can take a vehicle over, the island is small enough to cycle or even walk – the beaches are a ten-kilometre walk or cycle along the road.

Kilmory

REGION **West Kintyre**   LAT/LONG **55.909, -5.681**
GRID REF **NR 699746**   BEACH FACES **South**
ACTIVITIES **Swimming, walking, cycling, exploring the church**

A beach to visit for the views. Kilmory's beach is a perfect wild swim location with a wide, sandy, exposed beach and views of the Paps of Jura. Behind the beach, the Kilmory Knap Chapel and graveyard houses forty carved stones dating from the early Christian period to the sixteenth century. For the adventurous visitor, there is some great road and gravel cycling to explore in this area.

Access
There is very limited lay-by parking in Kilmory village. A trail path, which can be muddy, leads from the village to the beach. Kilmory is located on a peninsula of Kintyre accessed by single-track roads; do not park in passing places.

Oban and Lorn

A bustling seaside and fishing town situated in a west-facing bay, Oban is known both as the 'seafood capital of Scotland' and as the 'gateway to the Isles' due to the multiple ferry routes which set out from it to the Inner and Outer Hebrides, as well as some of the smaller Hebridean islands such as Lismore and Kerrera (an almost entirely car-free island). Oban has two outstanding beaches to delight in, including Ganavan Sands which offers water rated excellent by SEPA. This beach also has a Saturday morning parkrun, with views out to Mull and the Morvern peninsula – surely some of the best views you can get on a parkrun route.

How to visit

BY LAND There is a direct rail link from Glasgow to Oban, or alternatively you can change at Crianlarich if arriving by the Caledonian Sleeper from London. The Glasgow to Oban route also offers a dedicated cycle storage carriage on selected services. Additionally, regular buses run to many towns in Argyll and Bute, including the Citylink bus from Glasgow to Oban.

If driving, be aware of using passing places on single-track roads and look out for cyclists as many of these roads are also part of cycle networks. There are good road links from all major cities in Scotland, and a segregated cycle path (NCN Route 78) from Fort William to Connel, just north of Oban.

BY SEA Oban can be reached directly from many Hebridean islands. Please see CalMac for more information – *www.calmac.co.uk*

Ganavan Sands

REGION **Oban**   LAT/LONG **56.438, -5.469**
GRID REF **NM 862328**   BEACH FACES **North-west**
ACTIVITIES **Swimming, walking, trail running, cycling, snorkelling, stand-up paddleboarding, kayaking, joining in a parkrun, navigating a stone labyrinth**

Of the beaches in Oban, Ganavan Sands is the one to visit and one of the best for families. A gently sloping, sheltered, sandy beach with large car park and a slipway, this is a busy location but never feels crowded, and is also a safe place for children to swim. The perfect place to take in the views of the isles of Lismore and Mull as well as the Morven peninsula.

Ganavan Sands is one of the few SEPA-monitored beaches in Scotland and the water quality here has been rated excellent every year, making it a popular local swim spot. For further adventure, this is also the start of the Wild Kayak Trail that follows the Argyll coast, and also the coastal trails around the cliffs from the beach are often frequented by locals for trail-running and orienteering events. Along these trails you will also find a stone labyrinth. For those that prefer adventures on two wheels, there is a traffic-free cycle path from the beach to the town of Dunbeg, where the nearest shop is located. This a pleasant cycle, walk or jog and the route of the local parkrun on a Saturday morning.

Top tip
Visit Ganavan on a Saturday morning to join local swimmers for a wild swim and then take part in the parkrun from the beach at 9.30 a.m.

Access

This is possibly one of the most accessible beaches in Argyll. Frequent buses from Oban stop 300 metres from the beach. By car, from Oban town centre take the road following the coast north. The road ends in the beach car park, where there are two hours' free parking and public toilets.

Tralee Bay

REGION **Oban**   LAT/LONG **56.495, -5.422**
GRID REF **NM 894389**   BEACH FACES **South-west**
ACTIVITIES **Swimming, walking, cycling, mountain biking, kayaking, stand-up paddleboarding, running around a playpark**

Tralee Bay is a family-friendly, sheltered, crescent-moon beach and a favourite among local people; you will find wild swimmers here all year round. The west end of the beach is comprised of soft, golden sand with a playpark off the beach, whereas the east is pebbled. The beach slopes gently towards the ocean, with shallow, calm and clear waters, perfect for stand-up paddleboarding and families. Tralee Bay Holidays backs the beach, and in summer you can round your day off with fish and chips from the pop-up van (be sure to order in advance).

Nearby is the 308-metre Beinn Lora, which has great views of the beach and forestry trails and offers a lovely local walk or mountain bike. From the beach looking towards Beinn Lora keep an eye on the sky for sea eagles and buzzards. In the summer months the beach is often filled with moon jellyfish, but they do not sting and children often enjoy spotting them in the shallows.

Top tip
Visit Ben Lora Cafe & Bookshop for a raspberry scone and coffee and then wander down to the beach from the footpath opposite the cafe.

Access

From the Connel Ferry railway station (with direct connections to Glasgow) you can cycle over the Connel Bridge (over the Falls of Lora in Loch Etive) and join the segregated, flat NCN Route 78 cycle path all the way to the Ben Lora Cafe & Bookshop, where there is a sign to the beach. The cycle path carries on North to Ballachulish, and passes our next beach, Cuil Bay (overleaf).

There is free parking in a forestry car park at the foot of Beinn Lora, where frequent buses from Oban stop. Access the beach on foot via the footpath signed 'beach' from the cycle path.

The West Highland peninsulas and the road to Skye

Travelling north up the Scottish west coast, the beaches of the West Highland peninsulas can give those in the Bahamas a run for their money – if you have a thick enough wetsuit that is! Some truly beautiful beaches lie along these peninsulas, especially located between Oban and Mallaig. Head to the rugged remoteness of Ardnamurchan to discover the haven of Sanna Bay (p41) and stroll through beautiful forests and along bare coasts to Singing Sands (p42).

Follow the coast north to Morar via Glenuig, but be sure to take the scenic option. Turning off the A830 at Arisaig leads to a route scattered with beaches, each one its own paradise of silver sands and aquamarine water, with a backdrop of island silhouettes and even views of Skye's Cuillin Ridge on a good day. In good weather, these beaches are some of Scotland's most beautiful, dotted like jewels along just a few kilometres of coastline.

How to visit

BY LAND By car either take the Road to the Isles (A830), or the A828 from Oban with a ferry crossing at Corran. It is important to note that if travelling to the Ardnamurchan peninsula the main access route from Salen or Loch Sunart is a single-track, winding road for much of its length and can be a challenging drive.

There are daily Citylink buses and railway services from Glasgow which stop in Fort William. Additionally, the Caledonian Sleeper from London also stops in Fort William. From here change trains to go to Morar – this is a delightful rail journey, offering views of the north face of Ben Nevis and the opportunity to cross the Glenfinnan Viaduct. There is even the option to book the Hogwarts Express (also known as the Jacobite Steam Train) for Harry Potter fans of all ages. From the town of Morar the beaches are a few kilometres' walk away.

If travelling by bike, there is an excellent, segregated and flat cycle path between Oban and the ferry at Corran via the NCN Route 78; check out the Sustrans website for more information. The West Highland peninsulas are a popular destination for cyclists, with routes ranging from leisurely trails to challenging mountain bike routes.

BY SEA There are sailings from Corran and two ports on Mull: Fishnish to Lochaline and Tobermory to Kilchoan. Additionally, there is a passenger-and-bike-only ferry from Fort William to Camusnagaul.

Cuil Bay

REGION **Lochaber**   LAT/LONG **56.645, -5.299**
GRID REF **NM 978553**   BEACH FACES **South-west**
ACTIVITIES **Swimming, cycling, kayaking, spotting the wildlife**

Cuil Bay is a two-kilometre, south-west-facing beach comprising sand and shingle. Cuil is Gaelic for nook, and this beach lives up to its name – like others scattered along this coast, it is a wide beach cradled in a 'crab claw' of low hills on either side. This is a well-known beach and local swim spot and so is often busy, but it is great for kayaking and spotting seals. If you're driving north from Oban this is a nice little stop en route, but not worth going out of your way for.

Access

Take the sharp left-hand turn if heading north from Oban as you enter the tiny village of Duror. Follow a single-track road to the beach, where there is limited roadside parking. This beach often gets overcrowded with vehicles, so please respect parking along here and be aware livestock have access to the beach so you can often be sharing it with cows.

Easily accessible by bike from Ballachulish or Oban via the NCN Route 78 traffic-free cycle path, a flat and scenic cycle route suitable for families and inexperienced cyclists.

Camas nan Geall

REGION **Ardnamurchan peninsula, Lochaber**
LAT/LONG **56.684, -5.985**   GRID REF **NM 560617**
BEACH FACES **South-west**   ACTIVITIES **Hiking, cycling, discovering Ardnamurchan's history**

Camas nan Geall, meaning bay of the strangers in Gaelic, is a sandy bay with lovely views over Loch Sunart. The bay contains remains of a Neolithic chambered cairn at its head.

The Ardnamurchan peninsula is an area, like most of the Western Isles, that suffered from the Highland Clearances. For generations, local people had lived in small villages, paying rent and supplying armed men to the clan chiefs. But after the Jacobite uprising in 1745, clansmen and their families were evicted, their land sold and the tenants cleared to make space for the more profitable sheep rearing. Those evicted often left the area altogether, many for a new life abroad, but those that remained were moved on to less fertile land and assigned a croft. Crofts were a parcel of land designed to be too small to support a family, ensuring people had to find paid employment from which to pay rent. New crofting townships created at this time include Sanna, however the ruins of some settlements remain scattered across the Highlands; one of these former townships is Buarblaig, cleared in 1828, and its remains can be visited on the east slopes of Ben Hiant above Camas nan Geall.

As well as being a historic location, the beach is overlooked by a volcano. Ben Hiant is 528 metres high and the most prominent point on the peninsula. Formed around 60 million years ago, Ben Hiant epitomises the complex geology of the Ardnamurchan region, including quartz-dolerite, breccias, pitchstone, basalt lavas, cone sheets and Moine schist. These rock formations bear evidence of later sculpturing by glacial ice.

Access

Head down the Ardnamurchan peninsula on the B8007 and park at the forestry viewpoint which overlooks Camas nan Geall. Take the track down towards the sandy beach. Be aware there are sometimes cows on the beach.

Sanna Bay

REGION **Ardnamurchan peninsula, Lochaber**
LAT/LONG **56.744, -6.181**   GRID REF **NM 444692**
BEACH FACES **West**   ACTIVITIES **Swimming, walking, stand-up paddleboarding, kayaking, spotting the wildlife**

Sanna Bay is one of the most stunning beaches on the Ardnamurchan peninsula, with white sand and clear, turquoise water. The bay also offers some amazing views of the Point of Ardnamurchan and the Small Isles. This is a great spot for wildlife watching: look out for coastal birds and otters along the shoreline and keep an eye on the coastal cliffs for a chance of seeing white-tailed eagles. The machair here is also great for butterflies, dragonflies and damselflies.

Access

A car park rests at the edge of Sanna Bay with a short walk over the dunes to reach the beach; please bear in mind that the road along the Ardnamurchan peninsula is a winding, single-track road. Sanna Bay can also be accessed by a lovely coastal walk from Portuairk.

Singing Sands

REGION **Ardnamurchan peninsula, Lochaber**
LAT/LONG **56.7505, -5.908**   GRID REF **NM 612689**
BEACH FACES **North-west**   ACTIVITIES **Swimming, cycling, kayaking, stand-up paddleboarding**

The section of coastline which contains Singing Sands comprises a series of bays formed by large, rocky outcrops and breathtaking shoreline. Singing Sands, or *Camas an Lighe*, is hidden five kilometres from the nearest road access and backed by forest and woodland. Named Singing Sands after the sound the sand makes in the right conditions when the wind blows it over itself, this stunning section of coastline boasts soft, golden sand, crystal-clear water and rock formations which sit behind the beach. There are several bays along this coastline, and it is worth spending time exploring them all and finding a secluded nook to spend your day in.

This is an exhilarating swimming spot or stand-up paddleboarding location on a calm day, and there are some fantastic woodland tracks behind the beach which offer fun cycling opportunities for those on mountain or gravel bikes.

Access
From the village of Acharacle take the B8044 and then turn left. This road leads to the beach car park and start of the woodland trail leading to the beach. There is no car access beyond the car park and you will need to walk or cycle five kilometres through a forest via a gravel path, which is steep in places. There is a small sign pointing the way to the beach so you will not get lost. There is very limited parking at the start of the path, and it is likely to be busy in high season.

Top tip
Park in or catch the bus from Fort William to the town of Acharacle (which has public toilets and a cafe) and cycle in. Gravel or mountain bikes are advised.

Samalaman Bay

REGION **Glenuig, Lochaber**   LAT/LONG **56.832, -5.832**
GRID REF **NM 663777** BEACH FACES **North**
ACTIVITIES **Swimming, cycling, kayaking, enjoying a picnic**

Perfect for a day trip from Arisaig, Samalaman Bay is off the beaten track. Samalaman Bay is a small, sand-and-shingle beach with a beautiful view. Just the spot, hidden away, to sit peacefully and read a book on a sunny day, and afterwards continue along to discover coasts lined with woodland and small, sleepy beaches. This is a great beach destination to launch a kayak from. After your visit, follow the rocky coastline around to Glenuig Hall, taking in views of the Isle of Eigg.

Access
Easily accessible by car – there is limited car parking close to Glenuig Hall, and there is a local smokehouse and community shop nearby. This beach is best visited at a higher tide.

1

2

Traigh

REGION **Arisaig, Lochaber**   LAT/LONG **56.947, -5.855**   GRID REF **NM 656906**   BEACH FACES **North-west**
ACTIVITIES **Swimming, kayaking, stand-up paddleboarding, snorkelling**

The beaches between Arisaig and Morar are not to be missed. A mix of fine sand and shell with shallow, azure water and stunning views of Skye and the Small Isles, it cannot be emphasised enough how picture perfect and tropical Traigh, and all of this coast, feels – well, until you get into the sea that is!

All the beaches along this coast join up and contain rocky outcrops, making this shoreline a stunning place to kayak or stand-up paddleboard, or alternatively explore by snorkelling or rock pooling.

Access

There is very limited parking with a height barrier at Traigh Beach car park, located just a short walk south of the beach. Please refrain from parking on the grassy banks as these are very delicate. Walk along the road and then take a route across the field via a gate to reach the beach. There are many beaches that can be accessed from this car park, as well as several campsites all located within a short distance of multiple stunning beaches, making this a perfect option for visiting for a few days.

Camusdarach Beach

REGION **Arisaig, Lochaber**   LAT/LONG **56.959, -5.846**   GRID REF **NM 661918**   BEACH FACES **North-west**
ACTIVITIES **Swimming, kayaking, stand-up paddleboarding, snorkelling**

Camusdarach Beach is a long, wide beach of fine, white sand, backed by grass-covered dunes located just south of the estuary of River Morar. Enjoy these clear, sandy-bottomed waters while keeping an eye out for seals. All of this, combined with spectacular views out to the Small Isles of Rùm, Eigg, Muck and Canna, mean this is an incredible swim spot, with options to swim along the bay or around the rocks and to beaches on the other side. Some may recognise this coast from the film *Local Hero*, part of which was filmed here.

Access
Morar railway station is four kilometres away. There is a reasonably sized car park with a height barrier. It is a short sandy walk of around 300 metres to the beach.

Silver Sands of Morar

REGION **Morar**   LAT/LONG **56.962, -5.826**   GRID REF **NM 675922**   BEACH FACES **North-east**
ACTIVITIES **Swimming, stand-up paddleboarding, kayaking, enjoying a picnic**

The simply stunning beaches of the Silver Sands of Morar are in fact the narrow, fine, white-sand shores that line the mouth of River Morar. As these beaches line both sides of the freshwater river, the water may be even colder than the sea. However, outside holiday season, this is a perfect family spot for a picnic or relaxed day out.

Access
Morar railway station is just under two kilometres away. The easiest access is on the south shore: take the left turning off the A380 near Morar and take a right-hand turn soon after to reach a car park with height barrier. There are public toilets at the car park.

The Inner Hebrides (*Na h-Eileanan a-staigh*) is an archipelago off the west coast of mainland Scotland. The isles of Skye, Mull and Islay are the three largest islands, but make sure you take some time to visit the smaller ones as well. The beaches on these islands are some of the most unique and stunning beaches in Scotland.

These islands are steeped in history, culture, spirituality and religion. You will find many prehistoric structures, standing stones, churches and crofts on the islands, many of which are located on the coast and beaches, such as Kilnaughton Bay (p54), Kilchiaran Bay (p59), Kilvickeon Beach (p69) and Martyr's Bay (p77). Visiting these islands is an absolute joy, and the best way to visit is by ferry.

Various clan chiefs, including the MacLeans, MacLeods and MacDonalds, once had control of the Inner Hebrides, and there are still pockets where Gaelic is still spoken – many of the beach names are Gaelic or have been anglicised. The Highland Clearances of the nineteenth century had a devastating effect on many Hebridean island communities, the impact of which is still felt now. There are many examples of crofting ruins, where people were cleared from the land by landowners to make room for the more profitable sheep rearing.

INNER HEBRIDES

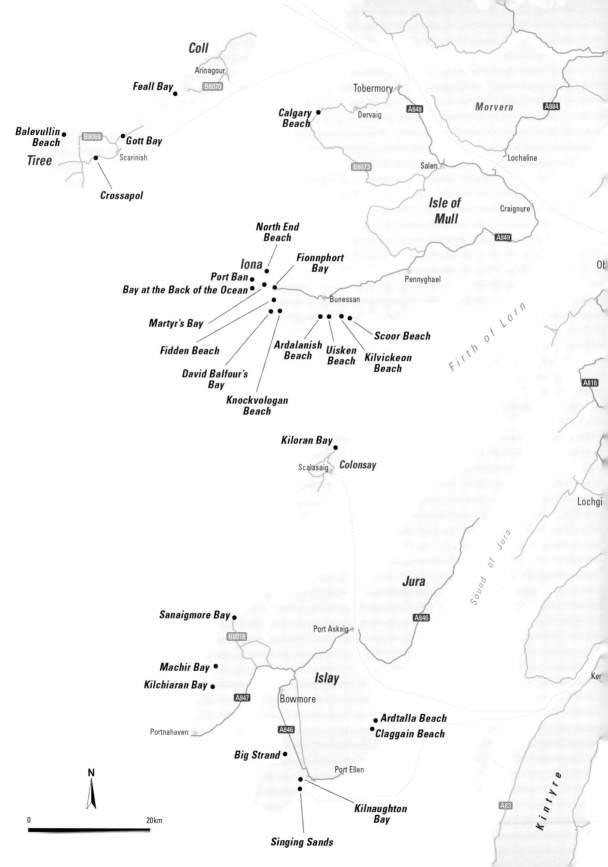

1 Ardtalla Beach

Southern Hebrides

Each of these islands has its own character, but all of them have something in common: visiting them leaves you feeling that you have truly travelled beyond the day-to-day world. You cannot help but fall in love with these islands, and the beaches on every single one are incredible.

Visit Tiree, the Land Below the Waves, to witness its unique quality of light, the warm local welcome and a surfers' paradise. Or Islay (*Ìle*), the whisky isle, and its huge array of distilleries as well as beaches. Also, do not forget Coll (*Eilean Cholla*) and Colonsay (*Colbhasa*) and the dreamy, sandy bays each offers. You are in for a real beach adventure whichever island you pick, and all of them are suitable for cycling around.

How to visit

BY LAND Direct trains and Citylink buses travel from Glasgow to Oban.

BY SEA Oban is known as the Gateway to the Isles for a reason: from Oban you can sail to all of these islands (excluding Skye) via CalMac services. The easiest way to visit Islay, however, is from Kennacraig in Kintyre. The best way to travel to these islands is by purchasing CalMac's Hopscotch ticket and just taking your bike.

Top tip
From the ferry to Tiree dial the Ring 'n' Ride bus to pick you up at the ferry port and take you to your accommodation. Or pre-book bike hire from Tiree Fitness and have a bike waiting for you on arrival.

Ardtalla Beach

REGION **Islay**   LAT/LONG **55.715, -6.036**
GRID REF **NR 466542**   BEACH FACES **East**
ACTIVITIES **Walking, stand-up paddleboarding**

A remote and hidden gem of a beach. Golden sands snake along this coast, with overhanging greenery and clear, shallow waters dispersed with rocky outcrops that only add to the tropical-island feel, almost as if you are in a rainforest. A beach to visit for a sheltered, peaceful walk, although be aware that cows often frequent the beach, so be careful to keep away from calves and bulls.

Access

Reaching Ardtalla Beach is a pleasant cycle or drive; a segregated cycle path can be found on parts of the route going east from Port Ellen. This route will take you past three of Islay's many whisky distilleries.

From the small car park (space for around three cars) south of the beach just after a bend in the road, walk through a cattle gate towards the farm then cut across a field to the beach. Beware of cows and bulls in the field and close all gates behind you.

Claggain Beach

REGION **Islay**   LAT/LONG **55.709, -6.040**
GRID REF **NR 463535**   BEACH FACES **East**
ACTIVITIES **Enjoying a picnic, relaxing with meditation**

Claggain Beach is a sheltered and pebbled shore, with a wonderful view back towards mainland Scotland. This pleasant beach is one to stop at for a picnic or to sit on the colourful, oval pebbles and enjoy the present moment.

Access

A pleasant cycle or drive from Port Ellen; part of this route has a segregated cycle path. On this route you pass three of Islay's whisky distilleries. The beach is a short walk from a small car park (just north of the beach before a bend in the road) with space for around three cars. From the road there is some grassland, bracken and a small, shallow stream to cross – using the riverbed stones is the best bet to try to keep your feet dry.

Kilnaughton Bay

REGION **Islay**   LAT/LONG **55.629, -6.217**
GRID REF **NR 347454**   BEACH FACES **East**
ACTIVITIES **Swimming, stand-up paddleboarding, kayaking, discovering Islay's history**
Ⓟ

A favourite beach with families, Kilnaughton Bay is one of Islay's most accessible beaches, and looks out east to Port Ellen. The bay has shallow, aquamarine water and soft, golden sands, making it perfect for a paddle. There are great views across to Carraig Fhada Lighthouse and the Mull of Kintyre.

The bay shares its name with Kilnaughton Chapel, which stands just above the shore of its west side, just past the modern cemetery. It is worth exploring the graves, some of which date back to the seventeenth century. Also be sure to venture inside the ruined chapel and visit the Warrior's Grave – this is a grave slab carrying a deep effigy of a knight in armour. Local legend states that the water that permanently fills the crook of his left arm is a cure for warts.

Access

This is easily accessible by car; head towards the Oa and park at the cemetery a kilometre and a half east from Cragabus. Walk around the cemetery to reach the beach.

1

2

3

Singing Sands

REGION **Islay**   LAT/LONG **55.618, -6.216**
GRID REF **NR 346441**   BEACH FACES **South-east**
ACTIVITIES **Listening to the sands singing**

A small, soft, golden-sand beach with sawtooth rocks between one and three metres high jutting out, Singing Sands is definitely a special place to visit. The rocks are great fun for kids to climb on, but also offer some shelter from the outside world. Supposedly, the sand sings as your foot dusts over the surface of the beach, earning the beach its name.

Although swimming is not advised here due to strong undercurrents, it is a great place to escape the worries of everyday life and admire the sheltered, crystal-clear water and the nearby Carraig Fhada Lighthouse.

Access

This is easily accessible by car; head towards the Oa and park at the cemetery a kilometre and a half east from Cragabus. Follow the road along the coast for nearly a kilometre. As you reach a row of houses before the lighthouse there is a signposted footpath around the back of them which leads you to the beach.

Big Strand

REGION **Islay**   LAT/LONG **55.662, -6.261**
GRID REF **NR 321490**   BEACH FACES **West**
ACTIVITIES **Walking, surfing, golfing, relaxing in a spa**

The Big Strand, also known Kintra Beach, is the longest beach on Islay at eleven kilometres long. This is an unsheltered beach with rolling waves and strong undercurrents, meaning it is not suitable for swimming; however, it is great for flying kites and building sandcastles. Even in the peak season there is always plenty of space on this beach due to its sheer size, but at the right time of year you can have the entire beach to yourself for hours. This is the perfect place for a long, refreshing winter walk, with the wind whipping away the cobwebs and any of life's worries, even if just for a moment.

Along with the Islay Airport, behind the dunes backing the beach is the impressive Machrie Hotel & Golf Links, a golf course with a hotel, restaurant, spa and even its own helipad – an upmarket spot to have a drink after your beach visit.

Access

This beach is fairly difficult to reach: the easiest way to access the beach is through the Machrie Hotel & Golf Links.

1 Kilchiaran Bay   2 Machir Bay   © Walkhighlands

Kilchiaran Bay

REGION **Islay**   LAT/LONG **55.752, -6.461**   GRID REF **NR 202600**   BEACH FACES **West**
ACTIVITIES **Discovering Islay's history**

If you felt Islay was a remote location before now, then heading to Kilchiaran Bay will leave you feeling you are truly heading into the back of beyond, with mainly forestry land and a few scattered farms and crofts surrounding it. You will rarely meet many people out here, and be prepared to manoeuvre into the nearest passing place when you do.

Kilchiaran Bay is a sunken, horseshoe bay with steep ground surrounding it, just off a road that used to be a slate quarry. This is supposedly the bay on which St Columba first stepped on Islay in AD 560, prior to founding the famous monastery on Iona. Overlooking Kilchiaran Bay are the ruins of Kilchiaran Chapel, and in the grass in front of the chapel is a stone marked with cup carvings.

Access
Buses from Port Ellen and Portnahaven stop in Port Charlotte, six kilometres from the beach. Take the single-track road heading west of Port Charlotte past the farm and chapel. There is no parking, so consider cycling or walking. Access the sunken, hidden bay from the chapel.

Machir Bay

REGION **Islay**   LAT/LONG **55.782, -6.456**   GRID REF **NR 206632**   BEACH FACES **West**
ACTIVITIES **Walking, hiking, sampling a dram at a whisky distillery**

Machir Bay, also known as Kilchoman Beach, offers up to two kilometres of stunning, sandy beach with cliffs to the south. Taking in the beach can be incorporated into a looped walk to the road just above it. It is actually possible to walk the headlands and cliffs to the south of the beach, following a track to get back down to the beach. Although beautiful, it is advisable to stay out of the waters here as the beach has warnings for strong undercurrents and a danger of drowning.

Near the beach is the Kilchoman Distillery which produces its signature peated single malt named Machir Bay. Nothing is better if you happen upon a beach in adverse weather than a dram to help you warm up again!

Access
There is a small car park at the end of the B8018, just above the beach. From the car park it is a short, easy trail through the grass to the beach.

Sanaigmore Bay

REGION **Islay** LAT/LONG **55.852, -6.416**
GRID REF **NR 238709** BEACH FACES **North**
ACTIVITIES **A place for reflecting**

A sheltered, beautiful beach, which is part of a series of bays. After admiring the crystal-clear waters you can head to the Outback Art Gallery and cafe on the road beside the beach, but do check opening times.

Located near the lay-by just before the art gallery is a memorial cairn for the 241 victims of the *Exmouth of Newcastle*, an emigrant ship wrecked while heading to Quebec from Londonderry in 1847. Of the 108 bodies recovered, most were women and children, with reputedly sixty-three of the victims being under the age of fourteen. They are buried under the green turf of Traigh Bhan.

Access

This is located near the end of the single-track B8018. Park in the small lay-by near the Exmouth Memorial Cairn. Watch out for bulls in the field as you walk to the coast and bay.

Kiloran Bay

REGION **Colonsay** LAT/LONG **56.103, -6.180**
GRID REF **NR 401980** BEACH FACES **North-west**
ACTIVITIES **Surfing, bodyboarding**

Colonsay's coastline is dotted with magnificent, sandy beaches, giving you plenty to visit and explore. The most popular beach on the island is Kiloran Bay: this large, sandy bay has views out to the Ross of Mull and is bordered by the peak of Carnan Eoin to the north-east. Be aware, however, of its strong currents. Take time to explore the caves at both ends of the beach, and at low tide head to the biggest cave at the north end to look for evidence of Neolithic use – it may be best to ask locals for directions to this. While on Colonsay, be sure to visit the local bookshop too.

Access

The beach is situated on the north-western coast of Colonsay with easy access from the B8086. There is a small car park on this road which overlooks the bay.

The sailing to Colonsay from Oban is approximately two hours and twenty minutes. Oban is well connected to cities throughout Scotland, and Glasgow, Edinburgh, Aberdeen and Inverness are all within a day's drive. There are also sailings from Kennacraig taking seventy minutes via Port Askaig on Islay. If you are travelling with an electric vehicle, a charging point is available at Argyll College in Oban. Colonsay also has a number of rapid charging points including at the CalMac ferry terminal in Scalasaig.

1 Balevullin Beach   2 Crossapol

Balevullin Beach

REGION **Tiree**   LAT/LONG **56.521, -6.955**
GRID REF **NL 954475**   BEACH FACES **North-west**
ACTIVITIES **Surfing, bodyboarding**

The white sand of Balevullin Beach (*Tràigh Baile a' Mhuilinn*) is situated in just the right place to capture the force of the Atlantic Ocean, providing a great beach for surfers. The local surfing school, Blackhouse Watersports, is located here, and it is well worth a visit to the family-run shack situated right on the beach, which offers equipment hire and surfing lessons. This is also a great place to stand high up on the grassy verge beside the beach and wave watch.

Access
Ferries from Oban take four hours and can carry cars. Located at the north-west end of Tiree, the beach is a twelve-kilometre cycle or walk on flat roads from the ferry terminal, taking the road to the north-west and following signs for Balevullin. To reach the beach turn right at the traditional crofting houses with thatched roofs. There is a small car park just above the beach.

Crossapol

REGION **Tiree**   LAT/LONG **56.487, -6.877**
GRID REF **NM 006438**   BEACH FACES **South-east**
ACTIVITIES **Surfing, windsurfing, bodyboarding, spotting the wildlife, paddling in waves**

Crossapol (*Crosabol*) is a long stretch of white sand backed by sand dunes with crystal-clear water. Although the waves here are smaller than those at Balevullin Beach, Crossapol is a favourite spot for locals to enjoy surfing and windsurfing. Be aware that there can be a strong pull along the beach, but this is a fun place to stay in the shallows and play in the waves.

Keep an eye out here for otter footprints on the beach, and if you're lucky you may even spot one. The local Tiree Trust offices are beside the beach, so check the ranger's Twitter page for local wildlife updates.

Top tip
Check out Tiree Polar Bears Facebook group for local swim meetups.

Access
The beach is just south of Tiree Airport, and walking distance from the local cafes and car park at Aisling's Kitchen at the Cobbled Cow. The beach is a six-and-a-half-kilometre cycle or walk from the ferry port, but be aware of the southwesterly prevailing wind, which at least makes cycling back to catch your ferry easier. If you pass the beach heading north-west, just as you round the end of the beach there is a trail leading you to the sand behind the rocks.

You can also contact the Tiree ranger to book use of beach-adapted wheelchairs – email *ranger@tireetrust.org.uk* or call 07391 239502.

Gott Bay

REGION **Tiree**   LAT/LONG **56.527, -6.789**   GRID REF **NM 050473**   BEACH FACES **South**
ACTIVITIES **Walking, windsurfing**

Gott Bay (*Got*) is a magnificent, six-and-a-half-kilometre-long, sandy beach encompassing the entire bay from the CalMac ferry terminal all the way to the Soa Cabins in the east. The beach is popular with windsurfers, and the Tiree Lodge Hotel looks over Gott Bay with its restaurant and bar.

Access
Gott Bay lies just north of Tiree's ferry port, which has sailings to Oban. There is a car park, toilets and a cafe at the ferry terminal. Buses which circle the island stop by the beach during school term time. The beach can be accessed at many points along the road behind Gott Bay, or directly from the ferry terminal.

Feall Bay

REGION **Coll**   LAT/LONG **56.594, -6.655**   GRID REF **NM 137540**   BEACH FACES **North-west**
ACTIVITIES **Swimming, walking, snorkelling, stand-up paddleboarding, discovering Coll's history**

Coll has many beaches to visit and explore, but unlike Tiree they can be harder to reach. Making the effort to get to them is worth it, and you will always be able to find a secluded and sheltered spot.

Feall Bay is the largest and most well-known beach on Coll. A well-photographed, north-west-facing bay, Feall Bay has clear, aquamarine waters and white sands. This is a beautiful spot to visit and swim at.

To the east end of the beach, you can walk up Ben Feall, a sixty-six-metre-high hill with fine views of Coll and Feall Bay. You will also find a memorial seat here for Kenneth Stewart, the last Laird of Coll. Another walk worth taking is a short walk from the car park of the B8070 to visit the Breachacha castles.

Top tip
To explore more of Coll with a tour look up the Oban-based tour company Basking Shark Scotland, which offers snorkelling and stand-up paddleboarding wildlife excursions to Coll.

Access
Coll is a two-and-a-half-hour ferry ride from Oban. From the ferry terminal, Feall Bay is around ten kilometres to the south-west; follow the B8070, then at the junction turn left and follow the road to its end, where there is a small car park. From here it is about a kilometre on foot to the beach, passing the start of a walk up Ben Feall.

Isles of Mull and Iona

The main thing to be said about visiting the beaches of the isles of Mull and Iona (*An t-Eilean Muileach agus Ì Chaluim Chille*) is that you are in for a real treat! Visit Mull for its breathtaking coastlines and hidden bays. Most of the beaches mentioned here (all except for Calgary Beach – p74) are located along the peninsula in the south of Mull, and from here you can catch the short ferry trip to the magical Iona.

The thirteen beaches listed here are some of the best beaches in this book. There are, however, more beaches to be found for those willing to take on pathless undergrowth. Part of the magic of these islands is in finding the beaches, and some have intentionally been kept hidden. That being said, these beaches are not all easy to visit, with many only accessible by bike or boat. This makes a trip to Mull and Iona a great beach adventure for a long weekend to a week.

How to visit

BY LAND Direct trains from Glasgow to Oban run regularly, and the Highland Explorer active travel carriage is available on this journey, which carries up to twenty bikes.

From Fionnphort, cars cannot travel to Iona, but it is a small enough island to walk or cycle around. The Iona campsite has good facilities and is suitable for families.

There are limited campsites on Mull, with only a couple in the south-west of the island which are not always open. Three beaches in this area offer overnight parking for campervans (with no facilities): Uisken Beach (p70), Ardalanish Beach (p70) and Fidden Beach (p74). Follow the signs on how to reach the landowner for permission and do plan ahead if camping or taking a campervan.

BY SEA Ferries from Oban to Craignure take approximately forty-five minutes. Alternatively, there are sailings from Lochaline to Fishnish and Kilchoan to Tobermory. Short ferries from Fionnphort on Mull sail to Iona.

Top tip
If you are not up for the sixty-kilometre cycle to Fionnphort from the ferry port at Craignure, stash your bike on a West Coast Motors Bus instead. Or take a car over with your bike and park at the overnight car park in Fionnphort.

Scoor Beach

REGION **Ross of Mull**   LAT/LONG **56.290, -6.167**
GRID REF **NM 422187**   BEACH FACES **South**
ACTIVITIES **Walking, mountain or gravel biking,
discovering Mull's history**

Scoor Beach (*Traigh Bhan Na Sgurra*) is a remote beach and well off the beaten track, as are many beaches on the southern coast of Mull. It is worth visiting both Scoor and Kilvickeon beaches on this trip as they are so close to one another: both are large, white-sand beaches with crashing waves, offering breathtaking views.

Scoor is beautiful, with its clear water, bays and caves to explore. There is also the secret Scoor Cave, which is difficult to find: there is no path and the going is very steep, but the views from the mouth of the cave are very dramatic. Within the cave the walls are covered in rock carvings said to date back to 2000–3000 BC. From here, there is also a walk of a few kilometres to visit the ruins of the town of Shiaba, cleared in 1845 in the Highland Clearances.

Access

Scoor Beach is not easy to access – the closest shop, toilets and pub are in Bunessan, around eight kilometres away. From Bunessan, take the A849 eastward and then take the first right heading south towards Loch Assapol. The road quality significantly decreases as it progresses and there is almost nowhere to park a car. The single-track road becomes gravel with large rocks and potholes, so consider reaching the beach by bike. After Loch Assapol the road deteriorates further, and should only be attempted in suitable vehicles or by bike. It should be noted that there is no parking beyond the sharp junction after the loch or at either of the beaches.

At the sharp junction by a farm and information sign, go left. At the end of the road there is a kissing gate to the left of a house; follow this rough path through the field, past the farm buildings and up the hill through the sheep field. At the top right-hand corner of the field, you will find a gate leading to another field and the top of the hill. From this vantage point you have a stunning aerial view of the beach and rocky coastline. On a clear day look out towards the mainland and isles of Colonsay and Jura. There is a steep track that leads to the beach from here.

Kilvickeon Beach

REGION **Ross of Mull**   LAT/LONG **56.291, -6.186**
GRID REF **NM 410188**   BEACH FACES **South-west**
ACTIVITIES **Walking, gravel or mountain biking,
discovering Mull's history**

Kilvickeon is a secluded, stunning beach with a rocky tidal island, Garbh Eilean, creating two bays as it juts out in the middle of the surf. This is a beach to visit for its large, sandy bay and rock pools, and depending on the weather this is a beautiful swim or paddle spot, with great aerial views of the beach as you descend the farm track. There are nearby walks to visit the town of Shiaba, one of the towns cleared in the Highland Clearances, as well as the ruined Kilvickeon Chapel and graveyard. Dun a Gheard, an Iron Age fort, also lies nearby.

Access

From Bunessan, take the A849 eastward and then take the first right heading south towards Loch Assapol. The road quality significantly decreases as it progresses and there is almost nowhere to park a car. The single-track road becomes gravel with large rocks and potholes, so consider reaching the beach by bike. After Loch Assapol the road deteriorates further, and should only

1

2

Knockvologan Beach

REGION **Ross of Mull**   LAT/LONG **56.292, -6.350**   GRID REF **NM 310196**   BEACH FACES **South-west**
ACTIVITIES **Swimming, walking, stand-up paddleboarding, kayaking, visiting the tidal island**

If you are lucky enough to visit Knockvologan Beach on a warm, sunny day you may think you have been transported to a beach in East Asia rather than Scotland. A beautiful and special location, this beach is more a series of beaches, grassland and tiny islands with their own beaches. Depending on the tide when you visit you can go out to these mini beaches and expanses of golden sand – a sheltered spot to explore by kayak, stand-up paddleboarding or swimming.

The highlight of a visit here for many is that on a low tide you can cross from Knockvologan to the tidal island of Erraid via a sandy beach between the two islands. This nicely leads you to David Balfour's Bay.

Access

This is a beach it might be best to visit by cycling, due to the difficulty in finding parking. From Fionnphort, take the road heading south and keep following it down towards Fidden. After the road bends to the east look for a right turn, which you follow down to a farm. There is no parking here, and there is a sign asking that cars do not block the road and farm vehicle access. From the farm descend a relatively steep and uneven path to the beach.

David Balfour's Bay

REGION **Erraid, Ross of Mull**   LAT/LONG **56.291, -6.373**   GRID REF **NM 295196**   BEACH FACES **South-west**
ACTIVITIES **Swimming, walking, kayaking**

David Balfour's Bay (*Traigh Ghael*) is a deep bay edged with pink granite, named after the character in Robert Louis Stevenson's novel *Kidnapped*. This beach can only be reached on foot at low tide, by boat or by kayak from Fidden Beach (overleaf) or Knockvologan Beach (above), due to its very remote and secluded location. It is worth the effort, as this is a magnificent beach – if going on foot from Knockvologan it can feel like a real adventure to cross the beach and disappear into the heather on the other side.

Access

This beach is only accessible by boat or on foot at low tide. Erraid is pathless, but just head west until the land runs out.

Fidden Beach

REGION **Ross of Mull**   LAT/LONG **56.308, -6.367**
GRID REF **NM 300214**   BEACH FACES **West**
ACTIVITIES **Swimming, paddling, kayaking**

Fidden Beach is a stretch of white sands interspersed with rocky outcrops which invite exploration. Just behind the beach is Fidden Farm Campsite, but it is not always open and has little or sometimes no facilities.

This is a great beach for kayakers and often used as a spot to take off from to kayak round to the tidal island of Erraid. When the tide is in, the pools between rocks make a nice swim spot.

Access

There is no real parking here, but Fidden is two kilometres away from Fionnphort, where there is ample parking. Please be mindful to not damage the delicate grass around the beach.

Fionnphort Bay

REGION **Ross of Mull**   LAT/LONG **56.326, -6.367**
GRID REF **NM 301234**   BEACH FACES **West**
ACTIVITIES **Experiencing a boat trip, paddling**

Fionnphort Bay is a beautiful little beach next to the village's ferry port with views across to the idyllic island of Iona. An iconic feature of the beach is a large boulder, deposited by glaciers in the last ice age, that is split down the middle as if by lightning.

For a full day out, from Fionnphort's ferry port you can join boat tours to visit the Treshnish Isles, including to Staffa and Fingal's Cave, or to spot the wildlife at sea. Round off your day with a stop at the pop-up seafood bar and treat yourself to some deep-fried scallops and chips.

Top tip
Come at sunrise or sunset to see the surrounding granite cliffs glow pink.

Access

This is very accessible: buses from Craignure stop a few times a day just by the beach. By car, take the main road all the way to Fionnphort and park in the overnight car park just before the ferry port, where there are also toilets, a cafe and a shop.

Calgary Beach

REGION **Mull**   LAT/LONG **56.578, -6.280**
GRID REF **NM 372512**   BEACH FACES **West**
ACTIVITIES **Swimming, admiring the art, kayaking, stand-up paddleboarding, venturing on a woodland walk**

Perhaps the best-known beach on Mull, Calgary Beach (*Cala Ghearraidh*) is the beach to visit on the island. The beach, which Calgary in Canada is named after, is a haven of white sand and shells, with clear, blue sea set in a wide, sheltered bay. A perfect place to visit with family or take a wild swim.

Calgary has a long and varied past: its name can be traced back to the Gaelic for meadow beside the bay or pasture. The bay was used to transport sheep to pasture to and from the Treshnish Isles, and up the hill from the beach are the ruins of a small village left during the nineteenth-century Highland Clearances.

Nearby you can visit Art in Nature and experience the sculptures and artwork in the woodland. Afterwards, just by the beach lies Robin's Boat, a small cafe with a roof made from an upturned boat hull, where you can buy some Isle of Mull ice cream.

1

2

3

1 Martyr's Bay **2** Bay at the Back of the Ocean © Walkhighlands

Access

This is easily accessible via the B8073: buses from Tobermory stop a few times a day at the southern end of the beach, where there are also a small car park and public toilets.

Martyr's Bay

REGION **Iona**   LAT/LONG **56.3292, -6.394**
GRID REF **NM 284238**   BEACH FACES **East**
ACTIVITIES **Paddling, walking, spotting the wildlife**

Martyr's Bay (*Traigh Ban Nam Monach*) is a small, sandy beach with a dark past: the beach is named after the killing of sixty-eight monks at this location in AD 806, when Vikings came ashore. In the past, this beach was used to bring coal from the Puffer boats that used to work the Western Isles from Glasgow.

If you are short on time, this is the perfect beach to visit while on Iona: the beach, though small, is beautiful and perfect for a paddle, and is conveniently close to the village of Baile Mòr and its amenities. Keep an eye out on the beds of flag iris here for the elusive corncrake – you may hear its call.

Access

The beach is just a few minutes' walk from the ferry terminal on Iona, just to the south. There is a shop near the ferry port. Ferries from Fionnphort run regularly; buses from Tobermory stop a few times a day here. Visitor cars are not permitted on the island, and so it is best to park at Fionnphort.

Bay at the Back of the Ocean

REGION **Iona**   LAT/LONG **56.327, -6.421**
GRID REF **NM 266234**   BEACH FACES **West**
ACTIVITIES **Walking, golfing**

The first reason to visit the Bay at the Back of the Ocean (*Camas Cuil an t-Saimh*) is for the crashing waves, in particular those at the Spouting Cave. Even on a relatively calm day, here you can witness water shooting into the sky. The second reason to visit is that this beach is comprised of one of the great delights of Iona: pebbles. Take a bag as you will be tempted to take home some of the beautifully coloured and smoothed pebbles. A real find are the yellowish-green stones of Iona marble, which is much prized for making jewellery.

Access

Buses from Tobermory stop a few times a day at Fionnphort, where ferries to Iona run regularly. Visitor cars are not permitted on the island, and so it is best to park at Fionnphort. From the ferry walk or cycle following the roads to the west coast of Iona, taking the road to the campsite. At the end of the road there is a gate leading on to the golf course and green with paths to the beach.

Port Ban

REGION **Iona**   LAT/LONG **56.333, -6.427**
GRID REF **NM 264244**   BEACH FACES **West**
ACTIVITIES **Swimming, walking**

Port Ban is a lovely, secluded beach, maybe Iona's prettiest, a short walk north along the coast from the Bay at the Back of the Ocean (p77). This is a perfect swim spot, sheltered from the crashing Atlantic waves beyond the rocky coastline and with steep cliffs either side of the white, shell sand. Head up on to the rocks for a view of the beach from above.

Access
Buses from Tobermory go to Fionnphort, where ferries to Iona run regularly; visitor cars are not permitted on the island. From the ferry port head south along the road, and then turn east towards Iona Campsite. At the end of the road, a small stile and gate through a fence lead to the beach.

North End Beach

REGION **Iona**   LAT/LONG **56.348, -6.389**
GRID REF **NM 288259**   BEACH FACES **North-west**
ACTIVITIES **Swimming, walking, spotting the wildlife**

A gem of Iona's coast, North End Beach can unsurprisingly be found at the north end of Iona. The beach follows the coastline round to the west, and is part of a series of dramatic, rocky shores, dunes and white, shell sand. This is a wonderful spot to explore, climb the rocks and swim in the sea. Keep an eye out for inquisitive seals too.

En route to the beach, it is worth walking up Dun I to take in the views of Mull, the Treshnish Isles and, on a clear day, Coll, Tiree and even Skye.

Access
Ferries from Fionnphort run regularly to Iona; buses from Tobermory stop a few times a day here. It is best to park at Fionnphort, as visitor cars are not permitted on the island. From the ferry port, follow the road north past Iona Abbey and follow to the road's end. There are bike locks here. Head north through the gate along the footpath. There are beaches on both sides of the footpath, but head to the left for North End Beach.

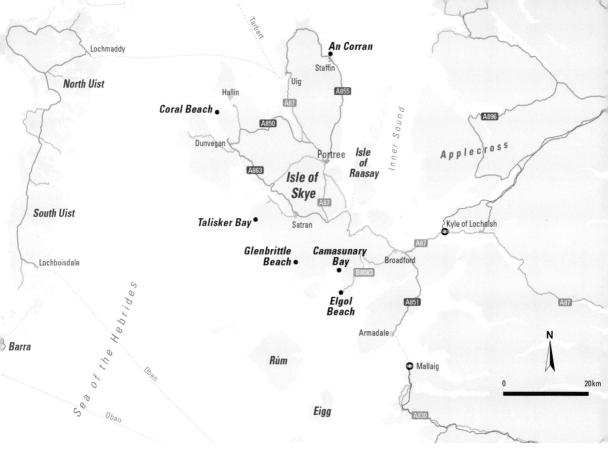

Isle of Skye

At eighty kilometres long, the Isle of Skye (*An t-Eilean Sgitheanach*) is the largest of the inner Hebridean islands. Skye instantly evokes images of extreme adventure and iconic landscapes, but also of magic, folklore and fairies. Skye is not a location to head to specifically for the beaches, but there are some unique gems to find on this island, from hunting for dinosaur footprints hidden among the rock lining An Corran (p84) near Staffin to walking into Camasunary Bay (p83), hidden in the foothills of the Cuillin Hills. From the bothy there, watch the sunset over the beach and stay the night.

Top tip
If visiting Skye and Arisaig, go in the off season. There is limited car parking at all of these beaches.

How to visit

BY LAND Skye can be accessed by car via either the Skye bridge or by taking the Road to the Isles (A830) and sailing from Mallaig. There are daily Citylink buses from Glasgow to Uig on Skye that stop in Fort William. By rail, take the train from Fort William to Mallaig and then sail.

BY SEA CalMac operate sailings on the Scottish mainland from Mallaig to Armadale. They also offer ferries to and from the Outer Hebrides at Uig, either from Lochmaddy on North Uist or Tarbert on Harris.

Additionally, you may sail to Kylerhea on Skye on the community-owned ferry *MV Glenachulish*, from Glenelg. This ferry is the last manually operated turntable ferry in the world, and the crossing via the Kyle Rhea strait a part

1 Elgol Beach

of the local heritage. If you can support this local business please do, and you can follow the ferry on Twitter. Due to the deep, narrow waters of the strait, there are chances to see basking sharks, dolphins, seals and otters.

Elgol Beach

REGION **Skye**   LAT/LONG **57.146, -6.107**
GRID REF **NG 516135**   BEACH FACES **West**
ACTIVITIES **Witnessing stunning sunsets, kayaking**
Ⓟ

Elgol Beach (*Ealaghol*) is located at the small village of Elgol in the south of Skye, at the tip of the Strathaird peninsula and on the shores of Loch Scavaig.

As well as having interesting rock formations and cliffs, this shingle and rock beach has breath-

taking and unmatched views of the Black Cuillin, and is a popular destination for photographers. When you catch a sunset here it is truly magical. This is also a kayak or boat launch spot to access Camasunary Bay (p83).

Access
Infrequent buses from Kyle of Lochalsh stop just outside the Elgol Village Hall. The B8083 is often backed up in the high season, and there is next to no parking except the car park at the southern end of the beach, although in summer many spaces will be taken up by coaches. However, it is an excellent (read: terrifying in places) cycle, starting from the Camasunary car park (see overleaf). From here you can cycle the six kilometres to Elgol Beach, along a fast-rolling road ending in a two-kilometre, very steep descent to the pier.

1 Glenbrittle Beach   2 Camasunary Bay

Camasunary Bay

REGION **Skye**   LAT/LONG **57.191, -6.119**
GRID REF **NG 511187**   BEACH FACES **South**
ACTIVITIES **Swimming, camping in a bothy, kayaking, sailing, hiking, mountaineering, mountain biking**

Located towards the south of Skye, at the foot of the Black Cuillin range, reaching Camasunary Bay (*Camas Fhionnairigh*) is in itself a mini adventure. An arduous but rewarding five-kilometre walk or challenging mountain bike ride leads you to this hidden, sandy bay. The intrepid explorer may want to carry on and climb the Black Cuillin, or alternatively if you arrive on a summer evening you can watch the sun set and spend a night in Camasunary bothy.

Camasunary bothy is a walkers' hut and is cared for by the Black Shed Project on behalf of the Mountain Bothies Association. The beaches on the west coast of Skye suffer badly from pollution of plastics and fishing gear, and so Camasunary bothy is piloting a Mini Beach Clean initiative in collaboration with Skye Marine Matters. Alongside day-long beach cleans, they are asking visitors to Camasunary Bay to carry out a few pieces of plastic on their visit. Bags can be found at the bothy.

Access
There is limited car parking on the B8083 just past Kilmarie, and from here there is a walk of approximately five kilometres to the beach. The start of the track has a National Trust for Scotland information board and donation box. This is a tough walk and even tougher cycle, up a steep, rocky path with 180 metres of ascent. The rewards are the views of the Cuillin Hills and beach.

Glenbrittle Beach

REGION **Skye**   LAT/LONG **57.202, -6.290**
GRID REF **NG 409205**   BEACH FACES **South-west**
ACTIVITIES **Hiking, enjoying a picnic**

Glenbrittle Beach (*Talasgair*) is a huge, wide beach of salt-and-pepper sand and shingle that sweeps along the foot of the Cuillin Hills. Stay at Glenbrittle Campsite and Cafe to enjoy easy access to the beach and mountains, with only a short drive to the Fairy Pools. On the campsite is Cuillin Coffee Shop, a cafe and shop that serves hot drinks, flatbreads, pastries and tray bakes. This is a great beach to let your kids loose, while you gaze up at spectacular sunsets and impressive views of the Cuillin Hills.

Access
A car park, as well as Glenbrittle Campsite and Cafe, are directly behind the beach.

Talisker Bay

REGION **Skye**   LAT/LONG **57.283, -6.457**
GRID REF **NG 314303**   BEACH FACES **West**
ACTIVITIES **Walking, surfing**

Misleadingly, Talisker Bay is not that close to the Talisker Distillery, but it shares the name of the original settlement here. A huge bay with large rocks along its borders and salt-and-pepper sand at the water's edge during low tide, this beach is worth the trip. The stunning views from here include the towering, sheer cliffs surrounding the north of the beach, an impressive, thin waterfall falling into the sea below and the mountains and glen that back the beach. This beach is also a popular spot for surfers.

Access

There is next to no parking near to the beach, so consider parking in Talisker – where there are public toilets and buses to Portree – and cycling the eight kilometres to the end of the public road. From the end of the public road the beach is a walk of a kilometre and a half down an accessible trail.

Coral Beach

REGION **Skye**   LAT/LONG **57.501, -6.637**
GRID REF **NG 223551**   BEACH FACES **West**
ACTIVITIES **Bathing, walking, kayaking, enjoying a picnic, visiting the tidal island**

Coral Beach is often high on people's to-visit list. A small beach entirely made up of maerl, a dried and calcified seaweed, rather than sand – if you imagine a beach of white, cream and pink-coloured hundreds and thousands sprinkles you won't be far off. There is a grassy hill behind the beach which offers a bird's-eye view of this coral point, surrounded with the aquamarine waters associated with Hebridean beaches. Depending on the tide, you can also visit the island of Lampay along the coral causeway.

Access

The road to the beach is a potholed single track, at the end of which is a small car park. The beach is a pleasant two-kilometre walk along a trail that passes through a cow field.

An Corran

REGION **Skye**   LAT/LONG **57.637, -6.205**
GRID REF **NG 491685**   BEACH FACES **North-east**
ACTIVITIES **Walking, exploring a museum, discovering Skye's history**

An Corran is Gaelic for point of land, and is located in the north of Skye opposite Staffin. The roads here offer some fantastic scenery, passing Kilt Rock and winding beneath the Trotternish ridge, a unique rock landscape formed by a series of landslides to form great tables, standing pinnacles and cliffs.

An Corran is not only an atmospheric, sandy beach, but also it holds a hidden surprise: search the rocks directly to the right of the walkway to find dinosaur footprints left in the rock. Amazingly, these prints, which are approximately 166 million years old, were only discovered in 2002. To find all seventeen footprints, it is best to visit at low tide and even better after a storm, which may remove some of the green seaweed which covers the footprints. Be warned that it is not easy to find them, but you can book a tour and find out more at the Staffin Dinosaur Museum located opposite the Kilt Rock and Mealt Falls viewpoint.

Access

Over winter, infrequent buses from Portree stop on the A855, and from here it is just over a kilometre to the beach. There is limited parking in a large lay-by to the side of a single-track road before the pier; follow signs to the beach and access it via a walkway. There is an information board about the dinosaur footprints. Remember to pack grippy shoes as the rocks are very slippery.

Situated roughly eighty kilometres north-west of the Scottish mainland, with the unrelenting Atlantic Ocean to the west, the coastline of the Outer Hebrides can be exposed to twenty-metre-high waves and gale-force winds. However, this land fails to be shaped by the environment, the gneiss rock a stalwart resister to time and erosion.

This 209-kilometre island chain is steeped in a rich and painful past, and you can immerse yourself in its history, language (the Outer Hebrides are a Gaelic-speaking stronghold) and local music. Visiting the west-coast beaches feels like you are standing on the edge of the world, and they provide views of jaw-dropping sunsets. Whether you want to walk kilometres of colourful machair, keep an eye out for rare birds or experience some of the best surfing, swimming and kayaking in Scotland, the Outer Hebrides is a great escape from everyday life. This coastline is littered with stories of shipwrecks, whisky smuggling and tales of hardship and history: these shores mark the roots of Jacobite uprisings.

The entire chain of Outer Hebridean islands can be visited in a single trip, from Vatersay (*Bhatarsaigh*) to the Isle of Lewis (*Eilean Leòdhais*). The ten islands included in this section can be crossed in only two ferry trips, otherwise utilising a series of causeways linking all islands but Barra to Eriskay, and Berneray to Harris (*Na Hearadh*). Although it is possible to drive between the islands, this route also exists as a walking and cycling route called the Hebridean Way – an experience not to be missed.

Top tip
If walking the Hebridean Way, make use of the bus network to skip the road sections. If cycling, do not be afraid to take detours from the waymarked route to visit the beaches and other areas of the islands.

OUTER HEBRIDES

Opposite Traigh Shiar **Overleaf** West Beach © Eilidh Carr

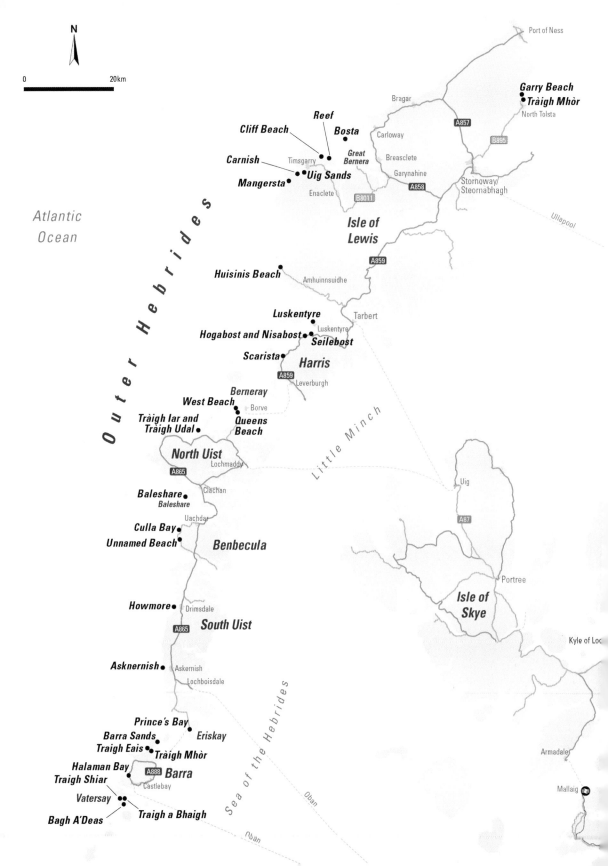

N

0   20km

Port of Ness

Garry Beach
Tràigh Mhòr

North Tolsta

Bragar

Reef

Cliff Beach   **Bosta**

Carloway

Breasclete

A857

B895

Carnish   **Great
Bernera**

Timsgarry   Garynahine

A858

Stornoway/
Steornabhagh

Mangersta   **Uig Sands**

Enaclete

B8011

Ullapool

*Isle of
Lewis*

*Atlantic
Ocean*

A859

Huisinis Beach   Amhuinnsuidhe

O u t e r   H e b r i d e s

Luskentyre   Tarbert

Luskentyre

Hogabost and Nisabost   **Seilebost**

Scarista   *Harris*

A859   Leverburgh

Berneray

West Beach   Borve

**Tràigh Iar and
Tràigh Udal**   **Queens
Beach**

L i t t l e   M i n c h

North Uist   Lochmaddy

A865

Baleshare   Clachan

Baleshare

Uachdar

Uig

Culla Bay

Unnamed Beach   *Benbecula*

A87

Howmore   Drimsdale

Portree

A865   *South Uist*

*Isle of
Skye*

Asknernish   Askernish

Lochboisdale   Kyle of Loc

S e a   o f   t h e   H e b r i d e s

Prince's Bay

Barra Sands   **Eriskay**

Traigh Eais   **Tràigh Mhòr**

Armadale

Halaman Bay   A888   *Barra*

Traigh Shiar   Castlebay

Oban

Vatersay   Mallaig

Bagh A'Deas   **Traigh a Bhaigh**

Oban

1 Halaman Bay

Vatersay and Barra

You will be forgiven for confusing photos of Vatersay and Barra's (*Eilean Bharraigh*) beaches with those of the tropics, and Barra is often jokingly referred to as 'Barra-bados' or 'Barra-dise'. These islands can be visited comfortably in a single long weekend, but if you are visiting Oban do plan in the time to sail over.

Often claimed to be Scotland's most beautiful Hebridean island, Barra offers an array of beaches for you to choose from. The island also allegedly has 1,000 species of wild flower and some of the rarest birds in Scotland, including the elusive corncrake, making it well worth the visit to this small island.

A journey across the 250-metre causeway from Barra to Vatersay will reward you with a long stretch of white sand and turquoise seas. For an aquatic adventure, you can embark on a boat trip in search of common and grey seals, dolphins and the occasional basking shark in the waters around the island. Whether you drive, rent a bike, hike or catch the bus, when you eventually arrive at Vatersay the stunning beaches will have you muttering 'how is this Scotland?'

How to visit

BY LAND From Barra, Vatersay can be visited via a causeway and Eriskay by ferry from Ardmhòr.

If travelling without a car, you can journey on foot following the Hebridean Way signposts or catch local buses to Vatersay or Ardmhòr from Castlebay. Alternatively, follow the Hebridean Way cycle route on the island. There is bike hire, including ebikes, from Barra Bike Hire at Castlebay.

BY SEA The main route to Barra is a ferry crossing of four hours and forty-five minutes by CalMac ferry from Oban, with daily summer sailings. On the approach to Castlebay, look out for the dramatic profile of Kisimul Castle, built on a tiny rocky outcrop in the middle of the bay. There is the option to purchase island-hopping tickets if you're planning to visit all the islands in one trip – see CalMac's Hopscotch 8 ticket. For the intrepid winter traveller, do bear in mind when planning your journey that there are frequent ferry cancellations due to weather.

> **Top tip**
> From the ferry call Cafe Kisimul (01871 810645) to order a curry ready for your arrival. Either sit in or, if the weather is suitable, enjoy it by the sea, overlooking the castle.

Bagh A'Deas

REGION **Vatersay**   LAT/LONG   **56.914, -7.530**   GRID REF **NL 634939**   BEACH FACES **South-east**
ACTIVITIES **Walking**

Bagh A'Deas is a beautiful, sandy beach on the south of Vatersay, backed by grassy hills and fields. It is truly away from the larger crowds, although Vatersay can never really be called crowded. Beware of cows in the fields or on the beach. It is not advisable to swim in the water due to it possibly being contaminated by excrement from the cows.

There is also a coastal walk which visits all three beaches on Vatersay starting at the cafe. There are details of the walk on the information board near the cafe.

Access
Limited parking, buses from Castlebay and toilets and showers can be found just by the seasonal Vatersay Hall Cafe, where the Hebridean Way also starts. From here follow the road south until its end and then head through several fields and gates to reach the beach. Be aware of the cows.

Traigh Shiar and Traigh a Bhaigh

REGION **Vatersay**
TRAIGH SHIAR: LAT/LONG **56.926, -7.541**   GRID REF **NL 629952**   BEACH FACES **West**
ACTIVITIES **Swimming, stand-up paddleboarding, sunbathing**
....
TRAIGH A BHAIGH: LAT/LONG **56.926, -7.535**   GRID REF **NL 633952**   BEACH FACES **East**
ACTIVITIES **Surfing, bodyboarding**
....

As you round the corner and glimpse Traigh a Bhaigh and Traigh Shiar it is hard to believe that you are still in Scotland. The far-flung island of Vatersay offers some truly breathtaking, golden-sand beaches, the jewel of which is the tombolo beaches of Traigh Shiar and Traigh a Bhaigh, offering both waves and shelter.

After passing through the much-photographed gate leading to the east-facing Traigh a Bhaigh, you can take a wild swim or even sunbathe in this sheltered bay and marvel at the clear, turquoise water. Facing west, Traigh Shiar is a great place to watch the waves or enjoy the surf. Both beaches encapsulate the peacefulness and remoteness of this most southerly inhabited Outer Hebridean island.

Access
Buses from Castlebay stop just by the seasonal Vatersay Hall Cafe, which lies between the two beaches and has public toilets and showers. Both beaches are easily accessible and a short walk from the car park just south of the cafe. There are also bike locks nearby.

Halaman Bay

REGION **Barra**   LAT/LONG **56.972, -7.521**   GRID REF **NF 646002**   BEACH FACES **North-west**
ACTIVITIES **Swimming, walking, surfing, bodyboarding**

Located on the west coast of Barra, Halaman Bay is a fabulous place to swim, surf and walk. The large, sandy beach, which looks out to the Atlantic Ocean, is arguably one of the best in the Hebrides. The stunning sunsets set this beach apart from others on Barra; on a cool summer's night, sit back and watch the sun drop beyond the watery horizon. When the sun has set, visit the Isle of Barra Beach Hotel which overlooks the beach; its restaurant serves a variety of dishes in the evening.

Additionally, there is a waymarked walk you can follow from the beach along the coastline to the south of the island, which takes you past a Second World War bunker and views of the remains of Macleod's Tower, dating back to the 1430s. A detour from the route takes you to the ruins of an Iron Age fort, Dun Ban.

Access
Buses from Eoligarry and Castlebay stop along the A888, which runs behind the beach. The nearest parking is in Castlebay, and from here it is a walk of two kilometres to the beach. There are public toilets at Castlebay's ferry terminal.

Tràigh Mhòr

REGION **Barra**   LAT/LONG **57.024, -7.449**   GRID REF **NF 694058**   BEACH FACES **East**
ACTIVITIES **Plane watching**

A Barra beach on many people's wish list is Tràigh Mhòr, also known as Barra Airport, situated towards the north of the island. The airport is the only airport in the world which uses a tidal beach as the runway. At high tide these runways are under the sea, so flight times vary with the tide. The beach is set out with three runways in a triangle, which always allows the Twin Otters that serve the airport to land into the wind. Poles are used to mark out where not to stray should a flight come in. As well as being a unique spot to watch planes come in and leave, the beach is well worth a visit in its own right.

Access
From the ferry, the beach is a pleasant four-kilometre cycle. Buses from Castlebay and Eoligarry stop just outside Barra Airport. There is limited parking just south of the airport.

Traigh Eais

REGION **Barra**   LAT/LONG **57.026, -7.454**
GRID REF **NF 691061**   BEACH FACES **North-west**
ACTIVITIES **Walking, surfing**

Traigh Eais is a long, sandy beach situated at the north-east tip of Barra, on the opposite shore to Tràigh Mhòr (p95) on the Eoligarry peninsula. Take in this open coastline from the tall sand dunes and look out west to the uninterrupted Atlantic Ocean.

There can be large waves along this beach, making an excellent wave-watching spot, or alternatively you can look out for planes arriving at the nearby Barra Airport. Head to the most northerly point of this beach for a great surf spot, where you may meet other surfers.

Access
Buses from Castlebay and Eoligarry stop just outside Barra Airport. There is limited parking just south of the airport. From here, a path through a gate and over the sand dunes leads to the beach.

Barra Sands

REGION **Eoligarry, Barra**   LAT/LONG **57.042, -7.421**
GRID REF **NF 713076**   BEACH FACES **North and east**
ACTIVITIES **Walking, kayaking, stand-up paddle-boarding**

Barra Sands extends around much of the northern and eastern coast of the Eoligarry peninsula on Barra. It is a beautiful spot, with white sands and clear water. From the slipway you can gaze at the stunning views of these Hebridean waters, and also of the small island of Fuday to the east of the Eoligarry peninsula.

Access
Buses from Castlebay stop just behind the beach. There are several access points to the coast from the single-track road running through the peninsula, including from the seasonal Barra Sands Campsite.

Opposite Prince's Bay

The Uists

With their stunning beaches which seem to stretch infinitely before you, these islands will leave you not quite believing that the scenery is real. On the beaches of the Uists, you will be spoilt for choice of spots, often nameless, to stop and swim or paddle. Almost the entire west coast of South Uist (*Uibhist a Deas*) is one unending beach, reminiscent of somewhere much more tropical than Scotland, bordered on one side by aquamarine seas lapping foaming, white surf, and on the other by colourful bouquets of machair. These are the best beaches for walkers, who can follow the Hebridean Way along the coast and machair. Additionally, head to the west and north coast of North Uist (*Uibhist a Tuath*) to find some truly incredible beaches.

You may be forgiven for not realising you had left South Uist when you step on to the island of Benbecula (*Beinn na Faoghla*), which sits along with Grimsay between the two Uists. The beaches and land feel very much the same as South Uist, however access to the long, beautiful beaches is easier here than on South Uist, with the road running close to the coast. If you are pressed for time head to Benbecula, where you will find the easier access gives you time to visit more beaches.

Those interested in local history will find much to delight them here as well: Eriskay is probably most known for the story of SS *Politician* and the books and subsequent films it inspired, *Whisky Galore*. The ship destined for the Americas carried among its cargo over 260,000 bottles of Scotch whisky. During a storm in 1941 the ship sunk off the coast of Eriskay at Rosinish Point, and locals took it upon themselves to help salvage the cargo. The local pub, Am Politician, is named after the ship and a perfect stop for a dram and a meal post glorious swim.

Machair is a Gaelic word meaning fertile, low-lying, grassy plains, and the habitat here is one of the rarest in Europe, only occurring on the exposed western coasts of Scotland and Ireland. The sand in the Outer Hebrides is largely made up of crushed shells heaped ashore by waves from the Atlantic Ocean. Over time the calcium-rich shell sand created these fertile Scottish grassland habitats, on what would otherwise be barren islands. To see the machair in bloom, the best time to visit is between late May and early September.

How to visit

BY LAND South Uist is connected by causeways to Eriskay, Benbecula, North Uist and Berneray. If travelling by bicycle, North Uist is small enough to visit for the weekend, and is ideal for leaving the car at home and exploring on two wheels.

BY SEA From the Scottish mainland, sailings from Oban and Mallaig go to Lochboisdale on South Uist. Ferries sail from Uig on Skye to Lochmaddy on North Uist.

To reach Eriskay, the ferry from Ardmhòr on Barra takes forty minutes – vehicle reservations are recommended.

To get to Berneray you can take an eighty-minute ferry ride from Leverburgh on Harris across the Sound of Harris. Be warned, this is one of the more dangerous crossings you will undertake – the Sound of Harris is full of islands, islets and rocks, and the route followed by the ferry is a roundabout one.

Prince's Bay

REGION **Eriskay**   LAT/LONG **57.074, -7.305**
GRID REF **NF 786104**   BEACH FACES **South-west**
ACTIVITIES **Swimming, paddling, stand-up paddle-boarding, kayaking, discovering Eriskay's history**

A short walk from the ferry port you will find Prince's Bay, which many consider Eriskay's most beautiful beach. Not only is this beach special for its clear, tropical-looking water, but also for its history: Prince's Bay is known as *Coilleag a Phrionnsa,* Gaelic for the prince's cockleshell strand, and is said to be where Bonnie Prince Charlie first set foot on Scottish soil. From here he headed to Glenfinnan and attempted to take the crown in the 1745 Jacobite Rising. Above the beach is a cairn commemorating the prince's landing.

Access
From Eriskay's ferry port, where buses from South Uist stop, the beach is a short walk along the road. There are also showers, toilets and a small car park at the ferry port. The Am Politician pub is two kilometres away.

Askernish

REGION **South Uist**   LAT/LONG **57.187, -7.422**
GRID REF **NF 725239**   BEACH FACES **West**
ACTIVITIES **Swimming, walking, discovering South Uist's history, golfing**

A beach for walkers, Askernish stretches around five kilometres along the west coast of South Uist, and is a great location to stroll along the machair. This is also a top spot for golf enthusiasts, with an eighteen-hole golf course overlooking the beach. The historical ruin of Cladh Hallan also rests just behind the beach.

Access
Buses can be caught to Askernish village from Benbecula, and from the A865 to Eriskay. Access to the beach is possible from several points along the Hebridean Way walking route. However, if following the route the path in places is not well maintained and can be overgrown. There are also sections where you are walking between farmland and the beach with fences either side; ensure you are carrying enough water and snacks as there is nowhere to purchase food or drink. If driving, take the west road from the town of Daliburgh and near the road's end there is a path that heads to the beach.

Howmore

REGION **South Uist**   LAT/LONG **57.310, -7.400**
GRID REF **NF 749373**   BEACH FACES **West**
ACTIVITIES **Swimming, walking, running**

A long, sandy, west-facing beach, Howmore is a perfect spot to watch the sunset. This beach is suitable for playing in the shallows, but keep an eye out for otters and compass jellyfish (which if the tide is out could be littered along the sand). From either Drimsdale or Howmore do take a look back at South Uist's highest peak, Beinn Mhòr, behind you. It is also worth stopping to see the old, thatched-roof crofts, with traditional stones around the roof to hold the thatch on in storms.

Top tip
Take water and snacks with you as the nearest shop is quite a good walk inland from the beach.

Access
This beach is a short walk from the bus stop in Howmore, where infrequent buses to Bornish stop. Head towards Howmore Church and just after you reach it take the path north, following

it until you come to a farm, just past a lochan with a castle ruin on an island within it. Head west through the field to the beach. Be aware of potential bulls in the field and do not camp on farmland. Otherwise head to Drimsdale and walk from there, following the Hebridean Way.

Unnamed Beach

REGION **Benbecula**   LAT/LONG **57.443, -7.398**
GRID REF **NF 763521**   BEACH FACES **West**
ACTIVITIES **Swimming, walking, running along the beach**

Seeing as the west coastline of Benbecula is pretty much all white-sand beaches, not all of the beaches are named. This particular stretch of coastline is not to be missed – it is simply unending flat, white sands. As this beach is just by the Hebridean Way, it is perfect for taking a break to walk barefoot along the wet sand, or enjoy a playful swim. Keep an eye out for jellyfish, however, in particular compass jellyfish.

Access
Regular buses to Balivanich can be caught on the road that runs along the back of the beach. The beach can be accessed at many points along this road, although there is limited parking at the north end.

Culla Bay

REGION **Benbecula**   LAT/LONG **57.460, -7.401**
GRID REF **NF 761542**   BEACH FACES **West**
ACTIVITIES **Swimming, walking, birdwatching, watching the sunset, enjoying a picnic**

A wide, curved bay lapped by rolling waves just south of Aird, Culla Bay is a simply stunning sandy beach. Backed by a horseshoe of sand

dunes and machair, it is a haven for the ground-nesting waders that return here to nest each year.

The Hebridean Way route takes you across this beach, so if walking or cycling nearby plan a stop here either for a stunning west-coast sunset or for a picnic. There are picnic benches near the road at the north of the beach, offering perfect views to accompany your rest.

Access
This is easily accessed from the road just behind the beach at either end (although the beach is not visible from the road). Buses to Eriskay and Balivanich can be caught on the B892. There is a small car park at the north end of the beach.

Baleshare

REGION **North Uist**   LAT/LONG **57.530, -7.390**
GRID REF **NF 776615**   BEACH FACES **South-west**
ACTIVITIES **Swimming, stand-up paddleboarding, kayaking, discovering North Uist's history**

A visit to the remote, bolthole island of Baleshare (*Baile Sear*), which is linked to North Uist by a causeway, offers some spectacular white, sandy beaches backed by sand dunes. This island is inhabited by around fifty people and supports a crofting community. The island is very flat, and is just twelve metres above sea level.

Access
The causeway to Baleshare is on the south-west of North Uist – a great detour if you are travelling along the Hebridean Way. From the causeway, the beach is three and a half kilometres away along roads and through fields. There is a small car park just behind the beach – take the turn before Baleshare Bothies, which has two glamping pods, and follow the road to the car park.

Tràigh Iar and Tràigh Udal

REGION **North Uist**
TRÀIGH IAR
LAT/LONG **57.662, -7.358**
GRID REF **NF 805761** BEACH FACES **North-west**
....
TRÀIGH UDAL
LAT/LONG **57.684, -7.327**
GRID REF **NF 827785** BEACH FACES **North-west**
....
ACTIVITIES **Swimming, walking, kayaking, cycling, discovering North Uist's history**

When visiting the north coast of North Uist you are struck by its incredible beaches – in fact, this entire coast is just sweeping, white-sand beaches that on a low tide reach out far into the crystal-clear Hebridean waters. Of the kilometres of perfect beach, two highlights are Tràigh Iar and Tràigh Udal.

Tràigh Iar offers a wide, long stretch of white sands backed by swathes of fertile machair. Visit in late spring and early summer for a colourful array of wild flowers. From the beach you look out on to the tidal island of Vallay (*Bhalaigh*) around two kilometres away. You can cross to Vallay from Traigh Bhalaigh near the forestry, however, this is not an easy trip and not for the unprepared. Vallay is a low-lying island that was once home to people despite now being uninhabited; the evidence lies in the visible ruins of Vallay House.

Tràigh Udal is a beach on the sandy Udal peninsula, just north of Sollas. As well as stopping off at the beautiful, sandy beach, take a walk up to the trig point to take in the views of this incredible coastline. The peninsula is one of the most important archaeological sites in the Outer Hebrides and is rich in both human and natural remains, bearing evidence of the people that have farmed this fertile machair landscape for 8,000 years.

Access
Buses that travel circularly around North Uist can be caught in the nearest villages, Sollas and Grenitote, on the A865. Limited parking and picnic benches are available at Grenitote Picnic Area, three and a half kilometres from each beach.

Queens Beach

REGION **Berneray** LAT/LONG **57.703, -7.212**
GRID REF **NF 895800** BEACH FACES **South**
ACTIVITIES **Swimming, walking, discovering Berneray's history**

With views back towards North Uist, a trip to Queens Beach can be combined with a visit to the Giant MacAskill Memorial. This commemorates Angus MacAskill, who was born in Berneray; at seven feet and nine inches, at the time he was the tallest man to ever live.

After your beach day, stop by the Berneray Shop and Bistro for a bite, or grab one of their seafood pizzas.

Top tip
Drop by the lovely Coralbox gift shop for a little something of this special island to take home with you. The Coralbox website also offers live camera footage of Bays Loch, especially good for witnessing an island storm without having to be out in it.

Access
The causeway connecting North Uist to Berneray lies in the north-east of North Uist. Follow the road to Borve and then head south-west, following the road until its end.

1 Tràigh Iar © Shutterstock/Natasa Kirin   2 Tràigh Udal © Douglas Wilcox   3 Queens Beach © Eilidh Carr

West Beach

> REGION **Berneray**   LAT/LONG **57.710, -7.221**
> GRID REF **NF 891808**   BEACH FACES **West**
> ACTIVITIES **Swimming, stand-up paddleboarding,**
> **snorkelling, kayaking**
>

West Beach is an all-time favourite beach, with five kilometres of sandy perfection. This beach is so picturesque that the Thai tourist board once used images of it to advertise their own beaches. Whether you want to swim in azure waters, admire the white sand or gaze out to the mountains of Harris and Lewis looming in the background, this isn't a beach to be missed.

Access

From the causeway connecting the island to North Uist, follow the road to Borve and park on the roadside. Alternatively, for the full island experience, from the causeway head towards John's Bunkhouse and park in the very limited car park just before reaching it. If it is a low tide, take off your shoes and socks and walk straight across this tidal sea loch, Loch Bhuirgh. If the tide is in, you can take the longer route around the bay. From here, cross the machair fields to the road. From the road there is a gate to a cow field with a gap in the sand dunes on the other side. Head this way to access the beach, but be aware of possible bulls in the field.

1

2

3

1 West Beach 2 Scarista © Walkhighlands 3 Horgabost © Walkhighlands

The Isles of Harris and Lewis

Contradictory to common sense, the isles of Harris and Lewis are one single land mass rather than two separate islands. Although a trip to these enchanting islands offers some of Scotland's most stunning beaches and the chance to be immersed in the islands' Gaelic culture, it is also a place to take the time to read about the forced Highland Clearances that have shaped the human history of these lands and coasts.

How to visit

BY SEA Sail from Ullapool on the Scottish mainland to Stornoway on Lewis, or from Uig on Skye to Tarbert on Harris. If you're heading to the isles from North Uist, take the causeway to Berneray and sail from Berneray to Leverburgh.

Scarista

REGION **Harris**   LAT/LONG **57.822, -7.061**
GRID REF **NF 997925**   BEACH FACES **North-west**
ACTIVITIES **Walking, golfing, photographing the stunning scenery**

Scarista (*Sgarasta*) is a huge, sprawling beach of golden sands and cerulean water, backed by moody hills. Scarista looks out to the north-west into the open Atlantic Ocean and has a wide expanse of sand and dunes between the main road and beach.

The best way to view Scarista (and on a clear day the Harris coastline, the Uists and even St Kilda) is to climb the 368-metre Ceapabhal, the westernmost summit of Harris. The hill sits on a peninsula jutting out with only a sliver of machair to connect it to the rest of the island, with a sandy bay in-between. The easiest way up is to park in Northton (check out the bakery at Croft36 while you're there) and walk from here.

This way you will even take in an extra sandy beach, Northton Beach, on the way.

Alongside Scarista is Isle of Harris Golf Course, often described as one of the most picturesque locations for a golf course in the world.

Access

The Hebridean Way runs from Leverburgh ferry port over the fells and along the beachfront; there is a path leading to the beach just past the village church on the A859. If you continue along the A859 you will encounter Borve Beach, and then Nisabost, Horgabost and Seilebost beaches. Buses to Tarbert and Leverburgh can be caught on the A859 just by the church.

If you're taking the Ceapabhal hill walk, access is via the village of Northton.

Horgabost and Nisabost

REGION **Harris**
HORGABOST
LAT/LONG **57.864, -6.981**   GRID REF **NG 047969**
BEACH FACES **North**
....
NISABOST
LAT/LONG **57.861, -6.991**   GRID REF **NG 040968**
BEACH FACES **West**
....
ACTIVITIES **Paddling, walking, bodyboarding, discovering Harris's history**

These two beaches are situated just south of Seilebost and Luskentyre beaches (overleaf) on the west coast of Harris, and sit either side of a small headland.

The fine sand of both beaches finds shelter in the island of Taransay, which lies opposite the beaches, and depending on the weather you can choose which to visit for the best shield from the wind. Horgabost shares the same crystal-clear, green-blue water and pristine sands as Luskentyre and Seilebost, but can be slightly more protected from the elements.

On the headland between the two beaches you will find Macleod's Stone, which has stood for over 5,000 years.

Access

Buses to Tarbert and Leverburgh can be caught on the A859, just by Horgabost Campsite. There are several campsites all within a kilometre of the beaches.

Seilebost

REGION **Harris**   LAT/LONG **57.870, -6.956**
GRID REF **NG 061973**   BEACH FACES **West**
ACTIVITIES **Walking, hiking, discovering Harris's history**

Seilebost is a sweeping swathe of sand, with swirls of water from the freshwater river mouth reaching across the beach. This beach is especially stunning to view from above, with the view extending out to nearby Taransay and Luskentyre. However, take care while walking on the beach itself due to quicksand and rapid incoming tides.

Maybe a lesser-known reason to visit this beach is to walk the Coffin Road from Seilebost on the west of Harris over to the east coast. During the Highland Clearances, landowners forcibly removed tenants from the fertile land they farmed on the west of the island to allow for more profitable sheep grazing. The tenants were relocated to the east coast, where the land was less fertile. Due to the shallow soil, graves could not be dug and so the recently deceased would be carried back west for burial, following the Coffin Road.

Access

If you're wanting to visit while walking the Hebridean Way, it is not easy to access the beach: unfortunately, high deer fences with no stiles prevent access between the walking route and the main road. Instead take a detour from the Way to Horgabost and follow the road from here.

If driving, there is no parking in the village of Seilebost; do not park on the school road. Consider using public transport to reach this beach – buses to Tarbert and Leverburgh can be caught on the A859 in Seilebost village.

Luskentyre

REGION **Harris**   LAT/LONG **57.893, -6.954**
GRID REF **NB 065000**   BEACH FACES **West and north**
ACTIVITIES **Swimming, walking, bodyboarding, sailing, kayaking**

Luskentyre (*Losgaintir*) is often voted one of Scotland's best beaches, and for good reason. A truly idyllic location and swim spot for all the family, this is probably Harris's best-known and most-visited beach. Luskentyre not only offers white sands and clear, azure waters, but also impressive views of the island of Taransay, the location of BBC's *Castaway 2000*. In the right Hebridean light, the moody hills which can be seen from the beach almost look purple.

If you want to explore further, it is possible to charter a boat to Taransay, which also has some amazing beaches, including a tombolo beach.

Access

There is very easy access from the car park at the north end of the beach, which has toilets and bus services to Tarbert and Leverburgh. Follow the trail along the sandy banks of the river to the beach.

109

1 Huisinis Beach © Kristin Main **2** Mangersta © Colin S Macleod **3** Carnish

Huisinis Beach

> REGION **Harris**   LAT/LONG **57.995, -7.092**
> GRID REF **NA 991120**   BEACH FACES **South**
> ACTIVITIES **Paddling, walking, enjoying a picnic**
>

Located on the far west of Harris, Huisinis Beach (*Hùisinis*) is a firm favourite. Popular for its remoteness and its arc of pristine, white sands, the blue waters of the beach are surrounded by grassy banks and rocky coastline. Beyond the main beach, there are several more sandy beaches to discover.

Huisinis Beach (also known as Hushinish), despite the winding journey to reach it, is great for families: the North Harris Trust manages a large beach hut called Huisinis Gateway, which is open all year round to provide information and a sheltered spot to picnic in when the weather turns.

Access
Reaching the beach involves heading quite a way down a winding, single-track road. Car parking and beach access can be found at the Gateway building, which has toilets and showers. There is a campervan site nearby.

Mangersta

> REGION **Lewis**   LAT/LONG **58.164, -7.089**
> GRID REF **NB 010310**   BEACH FACES **West**
> ACTIVITIES **Walking, surfing**
>

Mangersta (*Mangarstadh*), located on the northwest of Lewis, is a place to marvel at the strength of the Atlantic Ocean. The strong currents and waves mean that this is not a beach to swim at, but it is a popular surfing beach. If surfing isn't for you then enjoy the white sands or take a walk over the nearby grass-topped cliffs, where you can take in the views of the sea stacks in the distance.

Access
There is very limited parking area at a quarry off the main road just south-east of the beach. Take the road down to the beach. There is a glamping site nearby.

Carnish

> REGION **Lewis**   LAT/LONG **58.181, -7.056**
> GRID REF **NB 030325**   BEACH FACES **North-west**
> ACTIVITIES **Swimming, bodyboarding, wave watching**

Approaching from hills backing Carnish allows you to take in the views of the great Atlantic Ocean the beach boasts. The cliffs which point out to the sea shelter the beach slightly, taking the brunt of the impact from the waves, making this a great wave-watching spot. On calmer days, confident swimmers could swim here.

In the winter of 2019, Lewis Pugh, the UN Patron of the Oceans, visited Lewis to complete a training camp in preparation to swim a kilometre in a supraglacial lake in Antarctica. He invited local people to join him on the swims and beach runs. Carnish Beach, along with Reef Beach and the inlet at Uig Sands (overleaf) were some of his training grounds.

Access
Buses to Brenish can be caught at the intersection of the main road with the road to Mangersta village. There is no parking at the beach, however around four kilometres down the road is a quarry with a few spaces. To access Carnish, walk along the road until you reach a house with a private road. Do not enter this road – instead follow the 'to the beach' sign and head through a gate to your right to go up and over the hill. This is a bit muddy and uneven underfoot, with a steep descent to the beach.

Uig Sands

REGION **Lewis**   LAT/LONG **58.185, -7.028**
GRID REF **NB 045328**   BEACH FACES **East**
ACTIVITIES **Swimming, walking, wildlife watching, discovering Lewis's history**

Also known as Ardriol Beach, Uig Sands (*Tràigh Uige*) is a unique landscape of sweeping, white sands with freshwater rivers running along the coasts on either side. The sandy expanse of beach nearly disappears with the high tide, which mixes with the freshwater river. Be careful not to get caught out when it does.

On your way to the beach look out for the magnificent wooden statue of a chess piece. In 1831 the famous Lewis Chessmen were discovered at the beach; the Viking chess pieces were carved in Norway in the twelfth century, mostly from walrus ivory. The chess set was allegedly found in a small, stone chamber at the edge of the beach by Malcolm MacLeod.

They are kept in the British Museum and the National Museum of Scotland. From the statue there is a path out through the dunes to the outer beach – keep a keen eye out for sea otters.

Access
There is a campsite with a few parking spaces, as well as toilets and showers with an honesty box, just behind the beach. A trail leads from here to the beach.

Cliff Beach

REGION **Lewis**   LAT/LONG **58.220, -6.968**
GRID REF **NB 083363**   BEACH FACES **North-west**
ACTIVITIES **Surfing**

This impressive, sandy beach lives up to its name as it is surrounded by some of the highest cliffs on Lewis. Cliff Beach (*Camas na Clibhe*) is also a true surfing beach, with reliable surf

1 Uig Sands 2 Cliff Beach
© Colin S Macleod

all year round and on any tide. However, it is important to note it is not safe to swim here and there are strong rip tides: the beach faces directly into the Atlantic Ocean and receives the full westerly swell from the ocean.

Access
Infrequent buses to Garynahine and Brenish can be caught just before the turn-off for the single-track road leading to the limited car park overlooking the beach.

Reef

REGION **Lewis**   LAT/LONG **58.218, -6.938**
GRID REF **NB 101360**   BEACH FACES **North-east**
ACTIVITIES **Swimming, running, surfing, body-boarding**

This is an incredible beach! Reef (*Traigh na Beirghe*) is a huge, long, sweeping arc of white sands and clear, azure waters. On a windy day

escape being blasted by the sand (which can hit your legs at speed in the wind!) by taking to the unrelenting, rolling waves which provide the ultimate sea playground. On a calm day, challenge yourself to swim the length of the beach and run back, recreating some of Lewis Pugh's (UN Patron of the Oceans) training regime in 2019 as he prepared to swim in a supraglacial lake in Antarctica.

To the east of the beach, take in the towering cliffs; in the summer admire the machair here, which is full of colourful wild flowers and orchids.

Access
From the public car park it is a short walk to the beach – be prepared to get your feet wet as you cross on to the sand. Traigh Na Beirigh campsite, which has public toilets, overlooks the beach, but be sure to book in advance. Infrequent buses to Brenish and Timsgarry stop at the campsite.

Bosta

> REGION **Great Bernera, Lewis**   LAT/LONG **58.257, -6.882**   GRID REF **NB 137402**   BEACH FACES **North**
> ACTIVITIES **Swimming, bodyboarding, discovering Lewis's history, admiring the art**
>

Bosta (*Traigh Bhostadh*) is a fabulous beach located on the island of Great Bernera just off the north-west of Lewis. This beach is brimming with local interest, both historical and current. One of twelve installations created by the sculptor and filmmaker Marcus Vergette, the Time and Tide Bell is located among the rocks in the surf at Bosta. When the tide comes in the bell rings with each rising wave.

In 1993, a great winter storm blew in and revealed a settlement hidden and preserved beneath the sand dunes. The main settlement is believed to have been occupied around the sixth to ninth centuries, meaning they dated from the late Iron Age or Pictish period. Take a walk around a reconstruction of these houses to imagine what it was like to live on these coasts centuries ago.

This is also a wonderful swimming spot, and the beautiful beach's sand is backed by grassy dunes which provide shelter for when you are getting dressed afterwards. The facilities on offer here and easy access mean this is a beach to make a point of visiting.

Access

Great Bernera can be reached from Lewis via a bridge. A car park with public toilets, which is just alongside a Commonwealth graveyard, is a short walk from the beach. Overnight camping is permitted for a small donation. Infrequent buses to Garynahine also stop just down the road from the car park. From here there is a trail down to the beach.

Garry Beach and Tràigh Mhòr

> REGION **Lewis**
> **GARRY BEACH**
> LAT/LONG **58.367, -6.217**   GRID REF **NB 535498**
> BEACH FACES **East**
> ··
> **TRÀIGH MHÒR**
> LAT/LONG **58.362, -6.211**   GRID REF **NB 537492**
> BEACH FACES **North-east**
> ··
> ACTIVITIES **Swimming, walking**
>

These two neighbouring beaches sit on the north-east on Lewis. Garry Beach (*Traigh Ghearadha*) is a sunken bay north of Tràigh Mhòr, characterised by several outstanding sea stacks right on the shoreline. Tràigh Mhòr is a long stretch of golden sands, culminating at the north end in a steep, sunken bay. Similarly to many beaches on Lewis, sapphire waters make these beaches glorious swimming spots on a calm day. While you're here, be sure to take a visit to the Bridge to Nowhere, an abandoned project from the early twentieth century.

Access

The beaches are just over a kilometre away from one another, and can be reached by walking over the headland which separates them. Both beaches are approximately two kilometres away from the village of North Tolsta. Frequent buses to Stornoway can be caught from the B895 in North Tolsta. Both Garry Beach and Tràigh Mhòr have car parks, and the latter has public toilets.

If you feel a draw to the north, be sure to follow this instinct: the beaches in the north-west are some of Scotland's most spectacular and impressive. Vast, sandy coasts with mountain vistas as well as remote beaches surrounded by clear waters await any visitor here, and the journey to visit these beaches is some of the best driving to be found in Scotland.

Top tip
Check out the North Coast 500 app for ideas, audio stories and songs from each region as you drive through it. The best time to visit is May, as the tourist season will not have fully kicked off and the weather should (hopefully) be drier. Although it will still be cold at this time of year, it means there is less chance of midges ruining your trip.

THE FAR NORTH-WEST

Opposite and overleaf Achmelvich Beach

Wester Ross

You cannot go wrong if you have chosen to spend your Scottish beach holiday on Wester Ross (*Ros an Iar*) – find red-sand beaches, stories of biological weapons, hidden car-free gems and beaches with stunning views of the Torridon mountains and surrounding islands. Located in the north-west Highlands, the area is renowned for the scenic splendour of its mountains and coastline and its range of wildlife.

It should be noted that in the high tourist season this location is often overpopulated, so do plan in advance and consider visiting out of season.

How to visit

BY LAND Check out the North Coast 500 route, following the north coast from Inverness and leaving the route to reach Kyle of Lochalsh near Skye. There is also a rail option, joining Dingwall near Inverness on the east coast to Kyle of Lochalsh on the west coast. Strathcarron can also be reached by railway from Kyle of Lochalsh and Inverness, with a local bus service to Applecross. There is a bus service to Ullapool from Inverness.

There are good road links from the east along the A835 and via the Skye Bridge. Do note that the famous Bealach na Ba road is not suitable for larger vehicles and may not be available for use in winter conditions.

BY AIR Fly to Inverness from major airports across Britain, as well as selected locations throughout Europe. This is a great place to start a car journey from if not travelling through Glasgow or Edinburgh.

Sand Beach

REGION **Applecross peninsula**
LAT/LONG **57.472, -5.865**   GRID REF **NG 683489**
BEACH FACES **South-west**   ACTIVITIES **Paddling, discovering Wester Ross's history**

On a clear day Sand Beach packs a view, and is considered by many to be the best beach in the area. Look out from this shallow, sandy beach towards Skye. As you walk back along the beach, keep your eye out for a rock shelter – this is a Mesolithic dwelling used 9,500 years ago.

Access

Sand Beach is approximately eight kilometres north of Applecross village, and there is a small car park north of the beach with a short walk along a track leading to the coast. Applecross is not the easiest place to get to, but a journey you will not forget: the infamous road to Applecross village, Bealach na Ba (meaning pass of the cattle), is a steep, winding, single-track road that reaches heights of 626 metres. This road is not suitable for learner drivers, caravans, large vehicles or in snow/ice, and is signposted as such with an alternative route provided. If you dare to take this pass, and the weather is on your side, it offers views normally exclusive to Munro baggers.

Red Point

REGION **Gairloch**   LAT/LONG **57.651, -5.810**
GRID REF **NG 727687**   BEACH FACES **North-west**
ACTIVITIES **Swimming, walking, kayaking, body-boarding**

Slightly off the beaten track, Red Point (*An Rubha Dearg*) is worth visiting if you're looking for something a bit special. As the name suggests, the sand here is iron-red, distinguishing it from many other Scottish beaches. This secluded, untouched beach is backed by giant sand dunes and on a clear day it offers a panoramic view of Skye. There are no facilities here, so you will need to carry out everything you take in. Red Point has an otherworldly quality and feels like a special place, so be sure to treat it as such.

As you approach Red Point via the single-track B8056 there is a small car parking space and a lookout point by the car park – it is worth stopping to take in a bird's-eye view of the beach. If you want to explore further, there is a second, even more secluded red-sand beach 500 metres away over the point.

Access

If you follow the B8056 to its end you will find a small car park. There is a gate with a sign leading the way through a sheep field towards the sand dunes. There are, in fact, two beaches accessible from this car park: Red Point is the most northerly and most accessible. The walk from the car is under a kilometre, and follows a beautiful, small river surrounded by gorse. Pass through the sand dunes on to the beach.

Gairloch Beach

REGION **Gairloch**   LAT/LONG **57.717, -5.685**
GRID REF **NG 805757**   BEACH FACES **West**
ACTIVITIES **Swimming, golfing, enjoying a picnic**

Gairloch Beach (*Geàrrloch*) is a small, enclosed and sheltered stretch of golden sands with clear seawater – a perfect spot for families. This west-facing beach has beautiful views over Loch Gairloch, which is especially enchanting at sunset. There is a wooden walkway from the path to the beach to protect the delicate dunes and grass, but this also makes the beach very accessible. Gairloch itself is a great base for visiting this part of the Highlands, and its shops and cafes are just a short walk from Gairloch Beach.

Access

As you approach Gairloch village from the south there is free car parking at the Gairloch Golf Club alongside the beach, which has public toilets, and additional parking can be found at a viewpoint a short walk north of the beach. Buses to Gairloch can be caught from the golf club car park.

Big Sand

REGION **Gairloch**   LAT/LONG **57.737, -5.769**   GRID REF **NG 756783**   BEACH FACES **South-west**
ACTIVITIES **Swimming, walking, stand-up paddleboarding, kayaking**

A long, wide, white-sand beach with breath-taking views of the mountains in Torridon to the east and Skye to the south-west, Big Sand (*Sannda Mhòr*) is an absolute stunner of a beach. It is ideally placed between Longa Island and the huge sand dunes that back it, which provide shelter from the wind. This is a great stretch of coast for stand-up paddleboarding, kayaking and wild swimming with its shallow, clear waters, and even in the busier seasons the beach is long enough not to get crowded. For the intrepid winter swimmer, why not visit Big Sand for a winter swim overlooked by the snow-capped mountains?

Access
Beach access is via the Sands Caravan and Camping campsite, where a shop can be found. The descent from the sand dunes to the beach can be steep. The nearest public transport and parking can be found in Gairloch at the Strath car park, five kilometres from the beach; buses to Ullapool can be caught here.

Firemore

REGION **Poolewe**   LAT/LONG **57.833, -5.682**   GRID REF **NG 814885**   BEACH FACES **North-east**
ACTIVITIES **Swimming**

A favourite with the locals, Firemore (*Fhaighear Mhòir*) is a large, open beach with red sands opposite the Isle of Ewe. At very low tide it may be possible to cross to the island, but take care not to get stranded. Apparently the water at this beach is the warmest you will find in these parts of Scotland, due to the Gulf Stream. Although Scottish waters can rarely be described as warm, if this makes the thought of getting in easier then go ahead!

Access
Very limited parking is available at a small car park just behind the beach. The beach is a short walk away along a path opposite the car park. There is also a nearby campsite.

Slaggan Bay

REGION **Achgarve**   LAT/LONG **57.884, -5.643**
GRID REF **NG 841941**   BEACH FACES **West**
ACTIVITIES **Hiking, cycling, discovering Wester Ross's history, trail running**

Inaccessible to cars, Slaggan Bay is truly a hidden gem. Reaching it involves following a track for seven kilometres until you reach the west coast of this peninsula; look out for the ruined crofting village of Slaggan on your way. A deep, amphitheatre-like bay opens out. The beach is surrounded by a high, grassy bank and feels remote and hidden. As you wander on to the sands, you will realise that the sea-water here takes on a peaty quality, rather than the turquoise waters of other beaches in the area, due to the surrounding grassy banks. This is the perfect beach for a mini bike or trail-running adventure, followed by a secluded picnic.

Access
As this beach is difficult to reach via car or public transport, consider cycling from Mellon Udrigle beach car park, which is seven kilometres east of Slaggan Bay. Follow the road south for two kilometres until you see a signposted right-of-way path to Slaggan Bay. Follow the flat, easy-going track for five kilometres until you reach the beach. There is a rough, steep path down to the beach from the apex of the bay.

Mellon Udrigle

REGION **Achgarve**   LAT/LONG **57.902, -5.560**
GRID REF **NG 891958**   BEACH FACES **North-east**
ACTIVITIES **Swimming, stand-up paddleboarding, kayaking, photography**

Located off the beaten track, Mellon Udrigle (*Meallan Ùdraigil or Na Meall*) is worth the visit if just for the view. From these silver sands, gaze out on one of the finest beach views of the surrounding mountains to be found in Wester Ross. To the north-east you can spot the recognisable profile of Suilven near Lochinver and the mountains of Coigach, including a glimpse of the top of Stac Pollaidh. Then to

1 Slaggan Bay   **2** Mellon Udrigle   **3** Gruinard Bay

the south-east the views conclude with a glimpse of An Teallach. Once you've captured the perfect photo, this beach is also great for a dip, or even stand-up paddleboarding or kayaking.

This unspoiled beach boasts shallow, fine sand leading into the clear waters of Gruinard Bay (below). A stunning little beach with a wooden walkway to protect the sand dunes backing it.

Access

There is a small car park towards the north end of the beach, which fills up quickly, and a wooden walkway down to the sands. There is also a campsite nearby.

Gruinard Bay

REGION **Achgarve**   LAT/LONG **57.852, -5.453**
GRID REF **NG 952900**   BEACH FACES **North-west**
ACTIVITIES **Discovering Wester Ross's history**

Although this little, sandy beach may not seem one of Scotland's more impressive, Gruinard Bay's (*Eilean Ghruinneard*) draw lies in its past.

Looking out from this beach allows you to glimpse Gruinard Island, also known as the Island of Death. In the Second World War, the British government used the island as a site of anthrax testing, dropping the biological bombs on to sheep to test its lethality. In the early 1980s the Operation Dark Harvest environmental group started sending sealed bags of the contaminated soil from Gruinard Island to government buildings, calling on them to finally decontaminate the island. In 1986 the island was cleaned, and it was declared safe in 1990. The Island of Death was declassified in 1997 and there has not been a case of anthrax in the tested sheep on the island since 2007.

Access

The beach has a car park and wooden walkway down to it, but no other nearby facilities. Perfect for a pit stop en route north, to contemplate the beach's story.

Ullapool to Sandwood Bay

The beaches on this coast are considered some of Scotland's most picturesque, and include the otherworldly Achnahaird Bay, dramatic Oldshoremore Beach (p132) and possibly the most remote beach in the United Kingdom, Sandwood Bay (p133).

The geology and nature here are spectacular, and beaches offer truly WILD swimming, great surfing and even sea-stack rock climbing. This is a place for those seeking out bigger beach adventures.

As you leave Ullapool and head towards the far north of Scotland, amenities and facilities are sparse. Do plan for food and fuel stops. However, this is a highly popular tourist destination so consider visiting out of season.

How to visit

BY LAND These coasts are on the North Coast 500 route, and many of the roads are winding single tracks. This is also a popular location for cycle touring. There are limited public transport links, but buses from Inverness to Ullapool are available.

BY SEA Ferries from Ullapool to the Outer Hebrides run regularly. You can reach the north coast from Orkney via ferry to Scrabster, not far from Thurso.

Achnahaird Bay

REGION **Coigach peninsula**   LAT/LONG **58.067, -5.362**
GRID REF **NC 018135**   BEACH FACES **North**
ACTIVITIES **Walking, surfing, spotting the wildlife, photography**

Considered one of Scotland's best beaches, Achnahaird Bay (*Achadh na h-Àirde*) is well worth the journey to reach it. A north-facing expanse of flat, golden sand, the waves crashing against the low cliffs either side of the beach create a serene landscape and unique spot. Sand dunes and machair fringe the beach, and the view of Stac Pollaidh and other neighbouring mountains to the south-east makes this a truly beautiful place to relax. The sand dunes here support plant life of national importance, including petalwort (which isn't found anywhere else in Scotland), dune-slack liverwort, matted bryum and sea bryum. Most of the surrounding area is Inverpolly Nature Reserve, a haven for wildcats, pine martens and golden eagles, meaning this is the perfect destination for wildlife enthusiasts. You may also meet surfers and windsurfers enjoying this remote location.

Access

Take the single-track road west from the A835 at Drumrunie for nineteen kilometres. On reaching the village of Achnahaird, look for a sharp right with a sign for the beach. At the end of this road is a small car park. The beach is a walk of under a kilometre after you cross through the gate. To reach the beach you walk out on a grassy plane high above the water, with rocky outcrops and rock pools, which has a great view of the bay.

1 Achmelvich Beach   **2** Clachtoll Beach

Achmelvich Beach

REGION **Assynt**   LAT/LONG **58.170, -5.306**   GRID REF **NC 056249**   BEACH FACES **North-west**
ACTIVITIES **Swimming, walking, stand-up paddleboarding, kayaking, spotting the wildlife, fishing**

Achmelvich Beach (*Achadh Mhealbhaich*) is a small, perfectly formed bay, with brilliant white sand and clear waters. A great place for a short sea dip, it is also a popular spot for kayaking and, on a wild day, windsurfing. Fishing enthusiasts will also be pleased with this beach, where cod, haddock, whiting, pollack, saithe and mackerel are all common catches. There have also been sightings of porpoises, dolphins and the occasional minke whale here. However, the abundance of activities on offer means that this coastline can often be busy.

If you want to explore further, there is also a second, more secluded beach a short walk north from the car park.

Access
Infrequent buses to Ullapool and Drumbeg can be caught by Achmelvich Beach Youth Hostel. Achmelvich Beach has a large car park, free toilets, a campsite, bins and a ranger on-site.

Achmelvich Beach can be accessed by taking the North Coast 500 route on the A837 to Lochinver and then driving, walking or cycling the seven kilometres to the beach. Alternatively, if visiting from Achnahaird Bay (p128) you can, instead of returning to the A835, take the left turn heading north along the coast and travel along one of the windiest single-track roads the north-west of Scotland has to offer – this route is not recommended for caravans, motorhomes, larger vehicles or nervous drivers.

Clachtoll Beach

REGION **Assynt**   LAT/LONG **58.189, -5.335**   GRID REF **NC 040271**   BEACH FACES **South-west**
ACTIVITIES **Walking, spotting the wildlife**

Clachtoll Beach (*Clach Toll*) is similar to Achmelvich Beach (above), but with some stunning rock formations and a local walk out to the headlands, where you can find mountain views to the south. The gorgeous, white-sand beach makes for an amazing spot to visit – you may even spot the whale jawbone beside the public toilets. To round your day off you can grab a bite to eat at the pop-up Catch Toll fish and chip van in Clachtoll.

Access
There is easy access following the stunning and winding B869 along the North Coast 500 route. To reach the beach turn off into Clachtoll Beach Campsite and follow signs for the beach; eventually you come to a car park with seasonal toilets and bins. Infrequent buses to Ullapool and Drumbeg can be caught on the B869 just behind the beach.

Oldshoremore Beach

REGION **Sutherland**   LAT/LONG **58.478, -5.088**   GRID REF **NC 200586**   BEACH FACES **South-west**
ACTIVITIES **Walking, surfing**

Oldshoremore Beach, known locally as *Am Meallan*, is one of the most beautiful beaches in Scotland and often appears on lists of Britain's best beaches. Not only are the beach's white sands made up of eroded stones and crushed seashells, but washed with rolling, aquamarine waves. Oldshoremore is a dramatic beach accessed from high up on the sand dunes, allowing for a bird's-eye view of the rocky outcrops and expanse of sand. This makes an extra special spot for a stroll or picnic. Be aware at times of high tide there may be no sand showing.

Oldshoremore Beach is one of three sandy beaches connected by a rough coastal path.

It is separated from neighbouring Polin Beach by the Eilean na h-Aiteig headland, and further along the coast you then reach Sheigra Beach.

Access
From the A838, the beach is reached by following the B801 then turning north at Kinlochbervie down a single-track road which leads to Oldshoremore and steeply descends to the free public car park. There are bins and toilets located here. The beach is accessed to the left of the toilet block, following a path and then a very steep, uneven descent down to the sand dunes. Glamping pods are available nearby.

1 Oldshoremore Beach   **2** Sandwood Bay

Sandwood Bay

REGION **Sutherland**   LAT/LONG **58.538, -5.059**   GRID REF **NC 219652**   BEACH FACES **North-west**
ACTIVITIES **Hiking, running, gravel or mountain biking, surfing, sea stack climbing, thru-hiking**

Situated on the far north-west coast, Sandwood Bay (*Bàgh Seannabhad*) is thought to be the most remote beach in the United Kingdom and one of the most remote in Europe. The isolated location means you need to hike (or gravel or mountain bike) a nearly fourteen-kilometre round-trip to reach the bay along a well-maintained track through moorlands and along lochans. The final section of the walk brings you abruptly into view of the beach and cliffs. Despite the long walk in, you will be well rewarded for your efforts: the beach is dramatic and stunning. As you descend to the beach you are greeted by Am Buachaille (meaning the herdsman in Gaelic), a sixty-five-metre sea stack popular with climbers to the south-west of the beach. Powerful waves make this a spot that draws in surfers and adrenaline enthusiasts looking for something a bit different.

Access

There is a large car park at the start of the walk to Sandwood Bay located at the village of Blairmore. There are free toilets, bins and information boards. The walk begins across the road from the car park and is signposted. Although there are no facilities at the beach itself, there are places to lock up a bike before reaching the sand dunes.

Heading east along the far north of the country, follow a scenic coastal road to mainland Britain's most northerly point. Witness the landscape and weather change from a fjordic system dominated by south-westerly winds to tall cliffs and swathes of sand beaches. This change is also reflected in the place names, as they begin to shift from their Gaelic roots to Norse influence.

Do not stop when the land runs out – head even further north by taking a trip to the Northern Isles. The regularly overlooked Scottish regions of Orkney and Shetland are not two single islands, but each a group of islands with ferry links between them. Both have different histories and characters and are packed full of beaches, far too numerous to be covered in this guide.

THE FAR NORTH

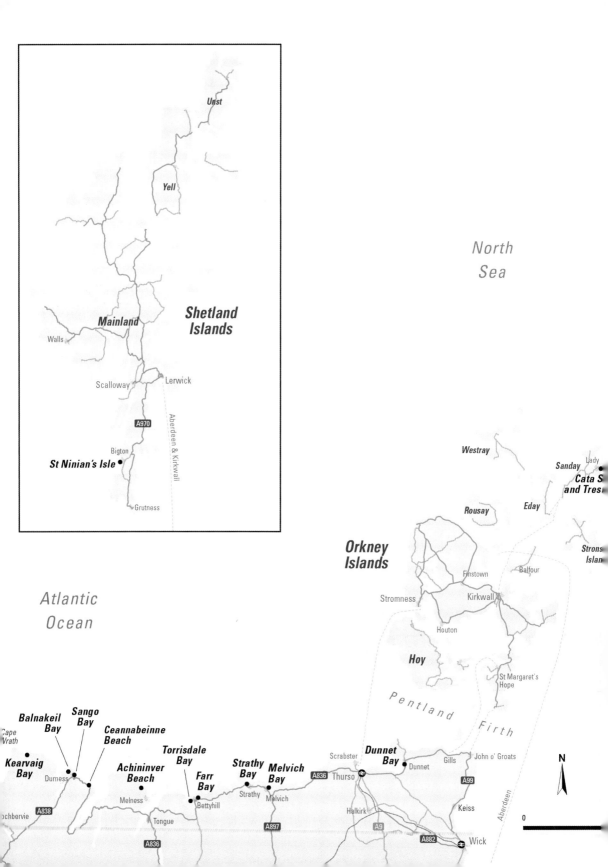

Unst

Yell

Mainland

Shetland
Islands

Walls

Scalloway   Lerwick

A970

Aberdeen & Kirkwall

Bigton

St Ninian's Isle

Grutness

North
Sea

Westray   Lady
                  Sanday
                           Cata S
                           and Tres
Rousay   Eday

Orkney
Islands
                Finstown   Balfour
                                          Strons
Stromness   Islan
                Kirkwall
Atlantic
Ocean   Houton

Hoy
                                    St Margaret's
                                    Hope
              P e n t l a n d
                                 F i r t h
                Scrabster   Dunnet
Balnakeil Sango   Bay
Bay   Bay   Thurso   John o' Groats
        Ceannabeinne   Dunnet Gills
        Beach   Torrisdale Strathy Melvich
Kearvaig   Achininver Bay   Bay   Bay   A836
Bay   Beach   Farr   Keiss
        Durness   Bay Strathy Melvich
Cape   A99
Vrath   Melness   Bettyhill   Aberdeen
ochbervie A838   Helkirk
                        Tongue   A897   A9
                A836   A882 Wick

N

0

1 Sango Bay

Durness to Dunnet

There is something awe-inspiring about reaching the north coast and knowing that, other than the Faroe Islands, there is only sea and ice between you and the North Pole. There is a unique quality to the light in this region at dusk. To catch some of Scotland's best sunsets, head to Balnakeil Bay (p140) or the viewpoint from Sango Bay (p143).

As you travel east the landscape changes, shifting from wild mountains and rocky coasts to increasingly large townships. The feeling of remote otherworldliness begins to dissipate, but in its place find tranquil bays at Achininver Beach (p143) and Farr Bay (p144), sandy stretches of beach at Strathy Bay (p147) and Melvich Bay (p147) and surfing at Dunnet Bay (p148).

How to visit

BY LAND There are bus links from Inverness to Durness and Tongue and rail links from Inverness to Thurso. Check local transport information for buses along the A836. This route is part of the North Coast 500, and has good road links along the A836.

Kearvaig Bay

REGION **Sutherland**   LAT/LONG **58.610, -4.944**
GRID REF **NC 290727**   BEACH FACES **North**
ACTIVITIES **Hiking, bikepacking, trail running**

Kearvaig Bay is an extremely remote bay, and a bit of an adventure to reach due to it not being accessible by private car. Backed by towering cliffs with amazing sea stacks before it, Kearvaig Bay, pronounced 'Kerwick', is a moody and atmospheric sandy beach. This is a good birdwatching location, where you may even see puffins.

Bear in mind that the area around Kearvaig Bay is owned by the Ministry of Defence and is used as a firing range when red flags are shown.

Access

The only facility at the beach is the nearby bothy. To reach this beach, cross the Kyle of Durness on the Cape Wrath ferry at East Keoldale Pier and hike along the extremely bumpy track for roughly twelve kilometres. The ferry takes only a few minutes and is approximately £7.50 (cash only) for a return trip. It may be best to turn up at the pier and have a friendly chat to find out when is best to travel over. Buses to Lairg can be caught in Durness.

For the truly adventurous, you can follow the Cape Wrath Trail from Sandwood Bay to Kearvaig Bay – be aware that this route is only for the very experienced hiker, and is considered the toughest long-distance route in Britain.

Balnakeil Bay

REGION **Sutherland**   LAT/LONG **58.578, -4.767**
GRID REF **NC 391687**   BEACH FACES **West**
ACTIVITIES **Swimming, hiking, kayaking, spotting the wildlife, discovering Sutherland's history**
Ⓟ

Of all of the beaches in this book, Balnakeil Bay (*Baile na Cill*) is consistently a favourite with many who visit. If you have clear weather, head to this far-flung headland to have your breath taken away. Hidden away on the far north coast of Britain, even on the approach you will not quite believe your eyes; you appear to walk out to kilometres of tropical beach, shaped in a crescent moon. The wide beach is comprised of white sand backed by an area of tall sand dunes covered in marram grass. For those looking to discover a bit of the bay's history, take time to explore the church ruins and graveyard close to the beach entrance.

To the north is Faraid Head, home to a military training facility and a naval gunnery range heading towards Cape Wrath – the walk to the end of Faraid Head and back is magnificent. This is definitely a beach for those looking for unspoilt beauty.

Access

This beach is situated two kilometres to the west of Durness – in the village you can find cafes, public toilets, a petrol station, shops and a campsite. If you are staying in the area, you can walk easily via the road leading west out of the village. Buses to Lairg can be caught in Durness. There are a few spaces to leave a car near the gate to the beach.

Sango Bay

REGION **Sutherland**   LAT/LONG **58.572, -4.741**
GRID REF **NC 407681**   BEACH FACES **North-east**
ACTIVITIES **Walking, camping, spotting the wildlife**

🅿 ♨ ♿

You truly feel like you have reached the end of Britain at Sango Bay. Surrounded by sheer cliffs on either side, crashing waves and views of the sea stacks to the east, this is a dramatic but lovely stretch of coast. There are two beaches here separated by a thin headland, at the top of which is a circular viewpoint.

Access
Access to the beach is through Sango Sands Oasis campsite at Durness, or over the headland at the south of the beach from the small car park just behind it. Buses to Lairg can be caught from Durness, and there is further parking in the village, which also has public toilets, cafes, shops and a petrol station.

Ceannabeinne Beach

REGION **Sutherland**   LAT/LONG **58.550, -4.677**
GRID REF **NC 442655**   BEACH FACES **North-east**
ACTIVITIES **Whizzing across a zip wire, exploring the nearby cave**

To the east of the village of Durness you will find Ceannabeinne Beach. Ceannabeinne means head of the mountains in Gaelic, but the beach was once known as *Traigh Alt Chail-geag*, translating as the beach of the burn of bereavement and death – according to local legend, this refers to the tragic story of a lady who was found on the beach, having died after falling in the burn.

The beach has spectacular views of the island of Eilean Hoan, which was once used as a burial site; prior to the Highland Clearances it was home to four families, but today the island is a nature reserve. In addition, thrill seekers will find the weather-dependent Golden Eagle Zip Line to the east of the beach which traverses the deep gorge.

Access
Access from A838 main road. There is a small car park opposite the zip wire for customers only, with space for a couple of cars – you can also park in the Parcheggio car park in Leirinmore (where there are public toilets and bus services to Lairg) and walk the three and a half kilometres to the beach.

Achininver Beach

REGION **Sutherland**   LAT/LONG **58.551, -4.452**
GRID REF **NC 572650**   BEACH FACES **North-east**
ACTIVITIES **Walking, enjoying a picnic**

A remote and beautiful beach off the beaten track, Achininver Beach is a wide and tranquil bay. It is best visited during low tide, when it offers great views north to the rocky cliff faces. As well as views out to sea, the view back up the beach is picturesque, with a burn running down the beach along rolling hills which are covered in yellow gorse in spring. There is also evidence on these hills of old crofting buildings.

Top tip
For a perfect picnic spot, head to the grassy ledge overlooking the beach with a thermos of tea and slice of cake.

Access
There is space for two or three cars in a small lay-by above the beach. From here it is a steep descent to the sand. The nearest facilities are in the village of Talmine, five kilometres away, where you will find a shop and bus services to Bettyhill.

Torrisdale Bay

REGION **Sutherland**   LAT/LONG **58.526, -4.241**
GRID REF **NC 695617**   BEACH FACES **North**
ACTIVITIES **Walking**

Torrisdale Bay is an impressive, wide, sweeping bay with windswept dunes. The whole of the beach and its dunes are a Site of Special Scientific Interest due to the rare plants and archaeological remains found here.

Reaching the beach is not straightforward, and is known as an easier beach to gaze upon from afar than to reach. This is due to the rivers on either side of the beach, the River Borgie and River Naver. However, those who make the effort won't be disappointed.

Access

This is not an easily accessible beach – the walk to reach here can be hard to follow so navigation skills are needed for the section between glens. It is easiest to park in Bettyhill (where there are public toilets) and walk back down towards the bridge over the river. In-frequent buses from Durness to Thurso also stop in Bettyhill. You then face a five-kilometre walk along the river to the beach over sand dunes.

Farr Bay

REGION **Sutherland**   LAT/LONG **58.533, -4.211**
GRID REF **NC 714625**   BEACH FACES **North-west**
ACTIVITIES **Walking, bodyboarding**

Farr Bay is a beautiful, tranquil beach. It almost feels surprising to find such a peaceful beach nestled so close to the village of Bettyhill, and only a short walk from the main road. Farr Bay is a flat expanse of golden sand. The bay is lapped by rolling waves and sheltered on all sides by low, grass-topped banks, with a bridge over the river to access the beach. This is a lovely spot to enjoy a walk, visit with the family or simply sit quietly, hidden away from the world.

Access

Park in the nearby village of Bettyhill, where you can also catch buses to Dounreay or Thurso. In Bettyhill there are public toilets, cafes and shops, and from here it is an easy walk on a path through fields to the beach.

1 Strathy Bay   **2** Melvich Bay

Strathy Bay

REGION **Sutherland**   LAT/LONG **58.566, -3.999**   GRID REF **NC 835658**   BEACH FACES **North**
ACTIVITIES **Walking, bodyboarding**

An award-winning beach, Strathy Bay's golden sands are flanked by sheer cliffs at one end and the River Strathy at the other. Wild flowers bloom just behind the beach during the months of May and June, while numerous caves and sea stacks are dotted along the coastline – perfect for getting off the beaten track and exploring. The jewel in Strathy Bay's crown is its views out over the Pentland Firth, which on a clear day are stunning.

Access
Infrequent buses to Thurso and Bettyhill can be caught from Strathy, just under a kilometre from the beach. By car, the beach is accessed by turning off the main A836 road once you reach Strathy and following the meandering, single-track road north-east, then turning north-west to follow the road past the cemetery to the car park, where there are public toilets.

Melvich Bay

REGION **Sutherland**   LAT/LONG **58.558, -3.913**   GRID REF **NC 887649**   BEACH FACES **North**
ACTIVITIES **Walking, surfing, salmon fishing**

Melvich Bay is an unspoilt, sandy beach backed by sand dunes and a large area of machair. The area around the River Halladale is abundant in wild flowers and bumblebees, making an idyllic stretch of coastline.

Those seeking a beach with plenty to see will find much to please them at Melvich Bay. For water-based activities, the beach area is well signposted and popular with surfers. For those wanting to immerse themselves in the past, there is a long history of human settlement in this area, including the ruins of four Iron Age roundhouses nearby. Also, Bighouse Lodge and estate is located to the east of the beach, at the mouth of the River Halladale and surrounded by water on three sides; salmon and trout fishing are on offer here. Bighouse Lodge was built for Louisa Mackay in 1765 and is a former home of the Chieftains of the Bighouse and Sandwood Chieftains of the Clan Mackay. There is a bridge over the river to visit it. It is also possible to rent the lodge and dine here for special occasions.

Access
Infrequent buses to Thurso and Bettyhill can be caught from Melvich, just under a kilometre from the beach. By car, turn east off the A836 in Melvich on to a track down to the beach, which has a small car park at its end. Alternatively, you can park in the village in a parking bay just by the turn-off from the A836 and walk less than a kilometre to the beach.

Dunnet Bay

REGION **Caithness**   LAT/LONG **58.615, -3.346**   GRID REF **ND 218705**   BEACH FACES **North-west**
ACTIVITIES **Walking, surfing**

Dunnet Bay is a beach for surfers, with some quite dramatic surf when the winds are high. It is also a great place for walkers, with the bay's golden sands stretching over three kilometres from Castletown to Dunnet. Backed by sand dunes, this sweeping arc of sand is one of the most northerly beaches in Britain. While you're here, be sure to visit the UK mainland's most northerly point, a short drive away at Dunnet Head.

Access
Frequent buses to Thurso can be caught on the A836 in Dunnet, just under a kilometre from the beach. Car parks are available at either end of the beach, just off the A836. Dunnet Bay Caravan Club Site rests towards the beach's northern end.

1 St Ninian's Isle **2** Tresness
© Walkhighlands

The Northern Isles

Lying off Scotland's northern coast, surrounded by crystal-clear waters, these are two archipelagos which are rather special places indeed. You really need to visit both Orkney and Shetland to fully appreciate these Northern Isles (*Na h-Eileanan a Tuath*). Don't rush your stay – each has a distinctive culture, natural wonders and several truly fascinating geological sites to take in.

The ferry to Orkney from the mainland takes under two hours, a journey which includes views of the iconic Old Man of Hoy, so if planning a north coast trip do factor this in. Orkney is a series of seventy islands linked by a series of ferries. As for beaches, you are spoiled for them here.

Scotland's most northerly archipelago is Shetland (the location of the BBC's *Shetland* crime drama television series) at sixty degrees north. Shetland has over 2,700 kilometres of coastline, 100 islands, natural harbours and clear waters. The coast offers a beautiful combination of dramatic cliffs and natural harbours, perfect for kayaking and sailing.

How to visit

BY LAND Direct trains travel from Inverness to Thurso, and from here you can get a bus to Scrabster. Aberdeen has direct trains from Edinburgh and Inverness.

BY SEA Visit Orkney by boat from Scrabster on Scotland's north coast to Stromness, or sail from Aberdeen to Kirkwall. Visit Shetland by sailing from either Aberdeen to Lerwick on an overnight ferry (which takes twelve to thirteen hours) or from Kirkwall on Orkney.

Cata Sand and Tresness

REGION **Sanday, Orkney**
CATA SAND
LAT/LONG **59.253, -2.530**   GRID REF **HY 697409**
BEACH FACES **South**

TRESNESS
LAT/LONG **59.237, -2.519**   GRID REF **HY 705389**
BEACH FACES **East**

ACTIVITIES **Swimming, kayaking, snorkelling**

The seventy islands which make up Orkney have an abundance of stunning beaches. The largest of Orkney's northern isles, Sanday, is reminiscent of the Outer Hebrides, with stunning beaches, sand dunes and machair resting at the fringes of fertile farmland.

Possibly the most spectacular sandy beaches in Orkney, and perhaps even in Scotland, are Tresness and Cata Sand. With three kilometres of glittering sands, Cata Sand is connected to Tresness by a thin peninsula. This peninsula creates a peaceful tidal bay, sheltered from the North Sea. The water has amazing clarity, making it a great swim location, although it is refreshing to say the least!

Access
From Kirkwall there is a ferry route to Loth on Sanday. To reach Tresness follow the road north until you come to a junction, then turn right and head east until you reach the B9068. Turn south and then east on to the B9069 to reach the Sanday Heritage Centre, where you can park in a large lay-by. From here it is just over a kilometre to the beach, following the road and then a path through a field. Tresness lies just south of Cata Sand, a lovely beach walk connecting them.

St Ninian's Isle

REGION **St Ninian's, Shetland**
LAT/LONG **59.970, -1.336**
GRID REF **HU 371207**   BEACH FACES **North and south**
ACTIVITIES **Swimming, bathing, kayaking, windsurfing, snorkelling, fishing, sailing**
WC

One of the most photographed beaches in Shetland, St Ninian's Isle is a striking location. The beach is a large, shell-sand causeway that links St Ninian's Isle to the south mainland of Shetland. This is considered one of the finest tombolo beaches in Europe, and is sure to impress all who visit.

The beach gives insight into the geology and geographical history that formed Shetland. Scotland was covered in a huge ice sheet which melted some 15,000 years ago. The rise in sea level from the melting ice meant that Shetland's valleys became submerged, creating instead the collection of islands we see now. If the water was drained away, we would be left with a landscape of hills and valleys. Islands such as Shetland are simply the tops of hills poking defiantly up out of the waves.

Access
Buses to Channerwick and Exnaboe can be caught in Bigton, half a kilometre from the beach. There are public toilets and a shop by the bus stop. The road to Bigton from both Lerwick and the ferry port at Grutness is a winding, single-track road with plenty of passing places. The beach is twenty-eight kilometres from Lerwick. The beach is part of a core path plan for Shetland – to find out more, pop into the local Visit Shetland office in Lerwick.

As you head east the Scottish mainland becomes more built up, with many of the beaches along this coastline resting alongside small towns and hamlets. Further south you reach the Moray coast and Aberdeenshire, where the beaches stretch out for kilometres along the coastline and provide surfing and dolphin-spotting opportunities.

North Berwick is a real hotspot not only for beautiful, sandy beaches, but also beaches offering something unique, including a tidal island crossing at Cramond (p176), views of the lighthouse on Bass Rock from Tyninghame (p180) or a stunning view looking inland of Tantallon Castle from Seacliff (p179).

EAST
COAST

Opposite Gullane Bents   **Overleaf** Cullen © Walkhighlands

Far North-East

This vast, open landscape is also known as the Flow Country. Named after the blanket bog in the region, the name comes from the Old Norse word *floi*, meaning wet or marshy. The far north-east of Scotland is rich in archaeological remnants, and the geological features of the Caithness coastline feature soaring sea stacks and raucous colonies of seabirds and seals.

As you head south towards the Dornoch Firth and Black Isle you will find lovely locations for family beach holidays.

It is important to note when planning a north-east coast trip that this area (along with Orkney and Shetland) experiences the haar between April and September. This is a rolling sea fog that descends on the east coast each year and often reduces visibility, including on the roads, and can cause temperatures to plunge.

How to visit

BY LAND There are excellent road, rail and bus links in this area, with railway stations located not far from many of the beaches between Inverness and Wick. Inverness has direct trains from Edinburgh, Glasgow, York and London.

BY AIR Inverness Airport has flights to major cities in Britain and Ireland, along with selected locations in Europe.

Sinclair's Bay

REGION **Caithness**   LAT/LONG **58.484, -3.125**
GRID REF **ND 342565**   BEACH FACES **East**
ACTIVITIES **Walking, surfing, spotting the wildlife**

Sinclair's Bay, known locally as Reiss Beach, is a stunning, white-sand beach with sixteenth-century castles at both ends. This peaceful beach is split in half by a stream, and has high cliffs and sand dunes flanking it. The south side of the beach is a useful shelter from the wind.

While you're exploring, keep an eye out for seabirds and whales among the surfers that frequent the waves – there have even been Orca sightings from this beach. The amazing light here means you can whale watch nearly all day long – in June the sun does not set until almost midnight. Although darkness enshrouds the beach in winter, it also means you may be lucky enough to see the Northern Lights.

Access

North of Wick, just by Reiss on the A99, regular buses to Thurso, John o' Groats, Wick and Inverness stop. Turn north-east off the A99 here to find car parking and beach access just past Wick Golf Club. Nearby Wick has shops, cafes and a railway station with direct services to Inverness.

Brora

REGION **Sutherland**   LAT/LONG **58.015, -3.840**
GRID REF **NC 913043**   BEACH FACES **East**
ACTIVITIES **Walking, spotting the wildlife, golfing**

Brora's beach is a small stretch of golden sand backed by a golf course. This rural beach is situated on the edge of the village of Brora and is great for wildlife watching. Keep an eye on the water for the fins of bottlenose dolphins, minke whales and grey and common seals. Brora is also a good spot to look out for Arctic terns – the terns arrive in May to breed on the dunes (please keep dogs on a lead and keep your distance to prevent disruption) and leave for the Antarctic in August. With benches on the seafront, this is a great place to enjoy a picnic and gaze out to the sea.

Access
Buses to Inverness, Golspie and Thurso stop just outside Brora's railway station, which has direct connections to Inverness. There is ample parking in Brora village centre, near the shop, where there are also public toilets and cafes. From here it is a walk of under a kilometre following the river path to the beach. There is also a walking route, signposted on local information signs in the village.

Embo

REGION **Sutherland**   LAT/LONG **57.911, -3.997**
GRID REF **NH 818930**   BEACH FACES **East**
ACTIVITIES **Bathing, walking, spotting the wildlife, enjoying a picnic**

A beautiful stretch of golden sand just north of the small village of Embo. The beach bends round to the mouth of Loch Fleet, overlooking the Dornoch Firth and its dunes, mudflats and beaches, which provide a habitat to a wide variety of birds, including terns, geese and waders. The lucky visitor may even spot a dolphin. Once you've had your fill of wildlife watching, you can explore the network of paths through the high sand dunes behind the beach.

Those visiting Embo may be interested in its brief departure from Britain: in 1998 the village declared itself independent from the rest of Britain for one day, to raise funds for a new community centre. The villagers even had their own currency, the Cuddie, which could be exchanged in the local pub for a measure of Clynelish Malt Scotch Whisky from the Clynelish Distillery.

Access
There is a small car park on the waterfront next to a slipway to the beach. Access is through the village, which has very narrow roads through housing and one-way systems, so are not suitable for large vehicles. There is a nearby campsite.

Dornoch Beach

REGION **Sutherland**   LAT/LONG **57.878, -4.013**
GRID REF **NH 806894**   BEACH FACES **East**
ACTIVITIES **Swimming, bodyboarding, enjoying a picnic, golfing**

Dornoch Beach is a popular beach which is well set up for visitors, families and holidaymakers. This beautiful, long beach is backed by dunes and is only a kilometre and a half from the bustling centre of Dornoch.

The sandy beach stretches south from the rocks at Dornoch Point, where there is shelter on a windy day, to the mouth of the Dornoch Firth. Dornoch Beach has been given Seaside Award status as a clean bathing beach and has a lifeboat station on-site, so you may see the volunteer team out training.

Access

Buses to Tain and Inverness can be caught in Dornoch on Station Road, just under a kilometre from the beach. There is a large car park on the beach, with easy walking access to the beach, and public toilets are located on Beach Road, which leads to the car park. A variety of cafes can be found in Dornoch. To the south of the beach are a holiday park and campsite.

You can book a free beach-adapted wheelchair by contacting the Dornoch Beach Wheelchairs team on 03007 704624, or messaging them through their Facebook page (*www.facebook.com/dornochwheelchairs*).

Shandwick Bay

REGION **Far north-east**   LAT/LONG **57.751, -3.917**
GRID REF **NH 860751**   BEACH FACES **East**
ACTIVITIES **Walking, discovering Shandwick's history, rock pooling**

Shandwick comes from the Norse *sand-vik*, and means bay. Shandwick Bay, which boasts a Seaside Award, is sandy with rock pools at either end and runs east from Balintore's harbour. For a lovely coastal walk, head to the west of the beach, where there is a good route to the Hill of Nigg with outstanding views over to Cromarty and the Black Isle.

There is plenty here for those that want to do a bit of sightseeing: at Balintore's harbour you will find a mermaid sat upon a rock pointing out to the sea. The rock itself is named Clach Dubh, meaning black rock in Gaelic, and the mermaid statue atop it is known as the Mermaid of the North, which commemorates a legend of a mermaid marrying a local man. Also, on the hill behind the beach are the remains of the famous Shandwick Stone, an impressive, nearly-three-metre slab dating to around AD 780.

Access

Regular buses to Tain can be caught on New Street, which runs through the village of Shandwick. A car park sits just behind the beach.

1 Dornoch Beach   2 Shandwick Bay © Walkhighlands   3 Rosemarkie Beach © Walkhighlands

Rosemarkie Beach

REGION **Black Isle**   LAT/LONG **57.593, -4.112**   GRID REF **NH 738578**   BEACH FACES **East**
ACTIVITIES **Bathing, walking, spotting the wildlife, enjoying a picnic, playing tennis, running around a playpark**

Rosemarkie Beach is a real favourite with locals and visitors alike. The beach boasts the community-run Rosemarkie Beach Cafe with plenty of lunch options and ice cream, as well as a playpark and tennis courts. Rosemarkie village is also only a short walk away with its shops and cafes.

For a full day out take a walk to Chanonry Point, one of the best spots in Scotland for dolphin watching. Alternatively, wander along the coastal walk to the north of the beach, checking out the Jurassic-like rocks along the coast which offer a natural climbing frame for children.

Access
Frequent buses to Cromarty can be caught on the High Street in Rosemarkie village, and buses to Inverness just up the road at the Fairy Glen Falls Beach Trail Head car park. Parking can be found on the road backing the beach as well as in the village, where there are public toilets. It is a short walk along the river to the beach and cafe.

Opposite Nairn

Moray Firth

The Scottish coastline south of Inverness at first might seem a little tame to those who are drawn to the dramatic, fjordic systems of the west coast. However, this region of Scotland offers picturesque harbour villages, huge swathes of sand and an array of wildlife. Visit for forest-backed beaches, long coastal walks and seal and dolphin spotting.

How to visit

BY LAND Nairn has direct trains to Aberdeen, which then has connections to Edinburgh, Inverness, Newcastle upon Tyne and London. There are road links to this region along the A90 and A96.

BY SEA Ferries from Aberdeen travel to Orkney and Shetland.

BY AIR Inverness Airport has flights to major cities in Britain and Ireland, along with selected locations in Europe.

Nairn

REGION **Inverness and Nairn**   LAT/LONG **57.592, -3.859**
GRID REF **NH 890574**   BEACH FACES **North**
ACTIVITIES **Swimming, walking**

Nairn's beach is split by the River Nairn, with wide, sandy beaches on either side. The east beach is known best for the wild swimmers that frequent it, and the water is SEPA monitored. Unfortunately, the water quality is only 'sufficient' – please read any information on the waterside regarding swimming, or on the electronic notice board which is updated daily with water quality.

To the east of the river is a walkway out to a lighthouse, offering a wonderful view of both beaches. With cafes both sides of the river, this beach is perfect for families and holidaymakers.

Access

Frequent buses to Inverness stop on the A96, just under a kilometre from the beach. There is a large car park to the east of the river, close to Nairn Lochloy Holiday Park. In Nairn town you will find public toilets by the shop on the A96.

1 Findhorn   2 Roseisle Beach © Shutterstock/JASPERIMAGE
3 Lossiemouth (West Beach) © Walkhighlands

Findhorn and Roseisle Beach

REGION **Moray coast**
FINDHORN: LAT/LONG **57.664, -3.617**   GRID REF **NJ 034649**   BEACH FACES **North**

ROSEISLE BEACH: LAT/LONG **57.674, -3.504**   GRID REF **NJ 100656**   BEACH FACES **North-west**

ACTIVITIES **Walking**

Findhorn is an expansive and open beach located near the mouth of the River Findhorn. A popular stretch on the Moray coast, the beach is lined with quaint, colourful beach huts and has wide views out to the North Sea. Nearby, the charming seaside village of Findhorn offers a bubbling atmosphere with pubs and restaurants along the riverfront and quay. But for all there is to explore around the beach, it is also a wonderful place for a calm walk at low tide, when the sand is exposed.

If you carry on walking south-east along this coastline towards Burghead (for approximately seven kilometres) you will eventually reach a real treasure – Roseisle Beach. A highlight of Roseisle Beach is the discarded remnants of anti-tank blocks strewn along the sand, and for further exploration the beautiful forestry trails which back the beach provide excellent walking and cycling.

Access
Buses to Forres and Elgin can be caught in Findhorn village on the B9011. Drive through Findhorn to its north-west tip to reach the beach car park, where there are public toilets. Be sure to park in a non-paying spot or book ahead for campervan or motorhome parking, or alternatively you can book a stay at the nearby Findhorn Sands Caravan Park.

Lossiemouth

REGION **Moray coast**   LAT/LONG **57.720, -3.301**   GRID REF **NJ 225708**   BEACH FACES **North-east**
ACTIVITIES **Walking, golfing**

Lossiemouth's beach is split into East and West beaches. East Beach is the one to visit, and is popular with surfers, however the footbridge to reach the beach has been closed since 2019 and is awaiting replacement.

Until the footbridge is replaced, Lossie-mouth's West Beach offers a five-kilometre, sandy strand with car parking, the Ponderosa Cafe and the striking Covesea Lighthouse.

Access
Regular buses to Elgin stop just west of the Moray Golf Club, a short walk from the beach. There is a car park at the egress to West Beach. There is also a car park at East Beach, with public toilets just up the road, but it's not possible to access the beach due to the closed footbridge. You can walk the kilometre and a half from East Beach car park to West Beach.

Aberdeenshire

Aberdeenshire has over 265 kilometres of scenic coastline to be discovered and enjoyed. Explore the impressive clifftops, alluring coves, idyllic sandy beaches, charming fishing towns and abundant wildlife under big skies and long horizons at these Aberdeenshire beaches.

There is also no shortage of activities to take part in here; the beaches are hotspots for surfers, windsurfers, kitesurfers and birdwatchers.

How to visit

BY LAND There are excellent railway links to Aberdeen from Edinburgh, Inverness, Newcastle upon Tyne and even London on the Caledonian Sleeper. There are railway stations along this coast and many local bus connections.

BY SEA Aberdeen has ferry connections to Orkney and Shetland.

BY AIR Aberdeen Airport has flights to major cities throughout Europe.

Opposite Inverboyndie Beach © Walkhighlands

Cullen

REGION **Moray**   LAT/LONG **57.693, -2.830**
GRID REF **NJ 505674**   BEACH FACES **North-east**
ACTIVITIES **Swimming, bathing, walking, surfing, diving and snorkelling, sailing, fishing, spotting the wildlife, golfing**

Cullen is a sandy beach overlooked by both the Cullen Viaducts and large rocks on the beach known as the 'Three Kings'. These four-metre-tall quartzite stacks are allegedly the gravestones of three Norse kings who died in AD 962 at the Battle of Bauds.

Cullen's water quality is monitored by SEPA, and it is a spot where you should keep an eye out for dolphins. To the east of the beach is a harbour and pet cemetery, and to the north you take a walk on the Portknockie cliffs path to view the famous Bow Fiddle Rock.

Access
Regular buses to Aberdeen and Elgin stop on the A98, a few hundred metres from the beach. There is free car parking just past the Cullen Viaducts, with the Coffee at the Kings cafe just beside it and public toilets behind the Cullen Links Golf Club. The Cullen Bay Holiday Park sits nearby.

Inverboyndie Beach

REGION **Banff and Buchan**   LAT/LONG **57.670, -2.551**
GRID REF **NJ 671649**   BEACH FACES **North**
ACTIVITIES **Swimming, walking, surfing, windsurfing, enjoying a picnic, running around a playpark**

Inverboyndie is a 700-metre sandy beach, considered one of the best surfing spots in the north-east of Scotland. This is a designated bathing water spot, and is a great beach for surfers, windsurfers, swimmers and walkers alike. With a large playpark and picnic benches just behind the beach, this is a great spot to enjoy with all the family.

Like many beaches along this coast, there is a good chance of spotting dolphins if you look long enough. After visiting the beach, why not explore the site of one of the many ancient castles in the area, such as Boyne and Findlater castles, some of which were built on the exposed coastline to protect against Norse raids.

Access
Regular buses to Aberdeen and Elgin can be caught on the A98, just over a kilometre from the beach. A large car park lies very close to the beach, behind the playpark. Banff Links Caravan Park is nearby.

Fraserburgh

REGION **Banff and Buchan**   LAT/LONG **57.683, -2.000**
GRID REF **NK 001660**   BEACH FACES **North-east**
ACTIVITIES **Swimming, bathing, running around a playpark**

Fraserburgh is a long beach of golden sand, stretching along the Aberdeenshire coastline to the point where the Moray Firth meets the North Sea. A large sand dune system backs the beach, which includes a salt marsh and reed beds. This is a haven for wildlife, including many species of wading birds. Lucky visitors might spot dolphins or even whales in the waters.

The beach is just a few hundred metres north of the centre of Fraserburgh, meaning while you dust the sand off your feet you can visit the town's Museum of Scottish Lighthouses and its harbour, which was once the largest working shellfish port in Europe.

Access

Frequent buses to Peterhead can be caught on Maconochie Road, running parallel with the beach. The beach is accessed down a short flight of steps at its north-western end. Here there is a car park, children's playpark, accessible toilets and the Tiger Hill Cafe.

Newburgh Beach

REGION **Fife**   LAT/LONG **57.308, -1.991**
GRID REF **NK 005243**   BEACH FACES **East**
ACTIVITIES **Spotting the wildlife**

The beach to visit if you want to see some seals! An abundance of seals live at Newburgh Beach, and the beach's colony is thought to be around 400. Be aware that for safety it is not advised to approach within 150 metres of the seals. The south side of the estuary is the best spot to watch the seals without disturbing them.

Once you've spotted some seals, this beach is also great for birdwatching – look out for eider ducks, oystercatchers and diving terns all nesting at Newburgh.

Access

Frequent buses to Aberdeen and Peterhead stop on the A975, a kilometre from the beach. The Ythan Estuary Beach car park lies half a kilometre away, with sand paths down to the river which leads to the beach.

Aberdeen Beach

REGION **Aberdeenshire**   LAT/LONG **57.161, -2.079**
GRID REF **NJ 954070**   BEACH FACES **East**
ACTIVITIES **Surfing, stand-up paddleboarding, admiring the architecture, visiting the amusement park**

Known for receiving the Seaside Award in 2013, Aberdeen Beach is just a short distance from the city centre. Take a paddle in the sea and walk the length of the promenade lined with shops, cafes, restaurants and attractions. On the seafront, you'll spot the Beach Ballroom, housed in a Category B-listed, art-deco building. The Beach Leisure Centre lies near the beach, along with the Linx Ice Arena and Codona's Amusement Park.

Access

Buses throughout Aberdeen stop on Links Road beside Queens Links Leisure Park. Roadside parking on the esplanade behind the beach. Alternatively, it is a short walk from the city centre. Public toilets available at the southern end of the beach.

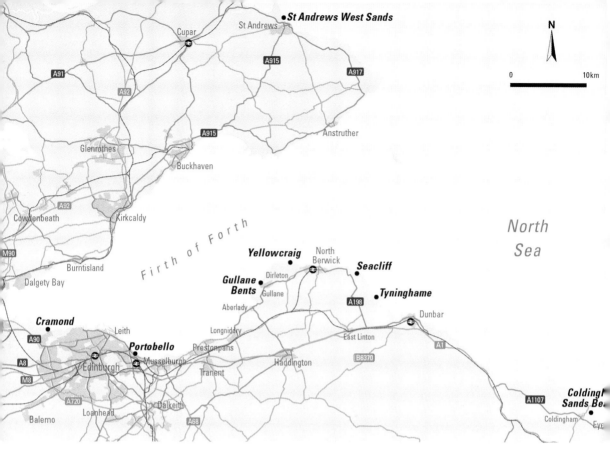

South-East

The south-east coast reaches from the Firth of Forth past Edinburgh along the North Berwick coast and all the way to the Borders. These are unique beaches with castle views, historic pasts and evidence of their roles during the world wars. There is plenty of choice if you're looking for golden-sand beaches, big horizons, wild-swim meetups and family days out.

They are also some of the most accessible beaches in Scotland: many are within reach of a day trip from Edinburgh, and several beaches offer both wheelchair access and beach-adapted wheelchair hire.

How to visit

BY LAND The A1 provides good road links throughout this region, with some beaches accessible by public transport. There are train stations at North Berwick and Dunbar, which both have direct connections to Edinburgh and Newcastle upon Tyne. Dunbar also has bus links to Berwick-upon-Tweed. Most beaches in this area have pay-and-display parking, but not all have toilet facilities nearby.

BY AIR Edinburgh Airport has flights to destinations, among others, throughout Europe and the United States of America.

1 St Andrews West Sands © Walkhighlands

St Andrews West Sands

REGION **St Andrews, Fife**   LAT/LONG **56.345, -2.805**   GRID REF **NO 504174**   BEACH FACES **East**
ACTIVITIES **Swimming, walking, spotting the wildlife, golfing, running in slow motion!**

St Andrews West Sands is most famously known as the filming location for the opening scenes of *Chariots of Fire*, but other than this attraction the beach also offers three kilometres of sand backed with dunes and the world-renowned St Andrews Links golf course. The beach holds many accolades, including a Keep Scotland Beautiful award.

Unusually for Scottish beaches, this beach is zoned to keep boats and people apart, and there are lifeguards on patrol during peak season. It should be noted that users must stick to footpaths in place on the beach as there is a dune stabilisation programme in place. The dunes here are part of the Firth of Tay and Eden Estuary Special Area of Conservation, and are of international importance due to the natural defence against the sea and the habitat they provide.

Access
Buses running from St Andrews to Dundee stop on Links Crescent, half a kilometre from the southern end of the beach. Parking can be found at the southern end of the beach, where there are also public toilets. Just over a kilometre away is the town centre, with a variety of cafes and restaurants as well as shops, museums and St Andrews Cathedral.

To book a beach wheelchair for use on St Andrews West Sands, visit *www.hamishfoundation.co.uk/beach-wheelchairs* or call 03000 122014.

Cramond

REGION **Edinburgh**   LAT/LONG **55.981, -3.298**
GRID REF **NT 190772**   BEACH FACES **North**
ACTIVITIES **Embarking on the tidal island walk**

Located in the Firth of Forth, one of the high-lights of this beach is crossing the 1.2 kilometre causeway to the tidal island of Cramond. It is extremely important to read the tide notices and tide times as visitors are regularly stranded by the incoming water – these are printed on a sign at the start of the causeway. Alternatively, you can text CRAMOND to 81400 to get a text containing safe crossing information by the Royal National Lifeboat Institution (RNLI).

Cramond Island, and the causeway itself, are covered in concrete structures from the world wars that have now been graffitied, giving the island a dystopian atmosphere.

Access
Buses throughout Edinburgh stop on White-house Road in Cramond. Pay-and-display car park next to beach, with public toilets. Cramond Bistro is just a short walk away.

Portobello

REGION **Edinburgh**   LAT/LONG **55.954, -3.108**
GRID REF **NT 308740**   BEACH FACES **North-east**
ACTIVITIES **Swimming, kayaking, stand-up paddle-boarding, coastal rowing, sailing, playing volleyball, wandering down the promenade, running around a playpark**

Located a few kilometres from Edinburgh city centre, Portobello is a charming seaside suburb with three kilometres of award-winning, sandy beach. The bustling promenade which lines the beach has plenty of independent cafes and restaurants, with picturesque Georgian and Victorian architecture and a boardwalk running alongside the beach. This beach is a popular spot with wild swimmers, with several meetups you can join.

The Portobello Sailing, Kayaking and Rowing Club is based here, along with RowPorty, a community-run coastal rowing club. There is no shortage of activities at this beach, and you will also find beach volleyball, places to sunbathe and playparks. This is a vibrant beach, full of people and families having fun.

Access
Located close to Edinburgh city centre, there are buses throughout Edinburgh which stop frequently on the B6415 behind the beach. There is a public car park on Bridge Street, and public toilets can be found on the promenade along with a variety of cafes.

Beach wheelchair hire is available at Portobello via *www.beachwheelchairs.org* or call 03006 660990.

Gullane Bents

REGION **East Lothian**   LAT/LONG **56.039, -2.842**
GRID REF **NT 476832**   BEACH FACES **North-west**
ACTIVITIES **Swimming, bathing, water sports, golfing**

Gullane Bents is a family-friendly, sandy beach with calm waters and glorious views out to the Firth of Forth. This beach is a real favourite location for wild swimmers, and on windy days the beach is also popular with wind-surfers and kitesurfers.

If you're after a relaxing visit, the beach is also a great picnic location, where you can look out for the small birds which populate the dunes backing the sand. To complete your day out, there is also a nearby crazy golf course.

Access
Buses throughout Edinburgh stop on the A198, half a kilometre away. The beach is a twenty-nine-kilometre drive from central Edinburgh. There is the pay-and-display Gullane Bents car park overlooking the beach.

Yellowcraig

REGION **North Berwick**   LAT/LONG **56.064, -2.779**
GRID REF **NT 515859**   BEACH FACES **North**
ACTIVITIES **Swimming, walking, enjoying a barbecue, running around a playpark**

Like many of the beaches along the North Berwick coast, Yellowcraig is an expansive and beautiful sandy beach. A natural cove beach with views to the nineteenth-century Fidra Lighthouse on the island of Fidra, which allegedly was the inspiration for Robert Louis Stevenson's famous tale *Treasure Island*, it is no wonder this is a popular place for coastal walks and rock pooling. Take a walk through the woods along the network of nature trails and find a sculpture designed in conjunction with local people, Disperse. There is also a barbecue area that can be pre-booked and a ranger service for the area, as well as a playpark behind the beach.

Around five kilometres away, North Berwick Bay is a flat, golden-sanded beach directly in front of the town and is a great place to explore after visiting Yellowcraig.

Access
To reach Yellowcraig by public transport, buses to North Berwick and Edinburgh stop on Main Road, a kilometre and a half from the beach. Yellowcraig is easily accessible by car, with a paid beach car park and toilets. There is a campsite nearby.

There is a wheelchair-accessible path and ramp to view the beach, and beach wheel-chairs can be booked in advance at both Yellowcraig and North Berwick – visit *www. beachwheelchairs.org* or call 03001 112112. There is also a hoist at North Berwick Bay.

Seacliff

REGION **East Lothian**   LAT/LONG **56.052, -2.637**
GRID REF **NT 604845**   BEACH FACES **North**
ACTIVITIES **Swimming, walking, enjoying a picnic, gazing at Tantallon Castle**

Seacliff is a real hidden gem. It is worth taking a walk up over the rocky headland of this sandy beach to find a tiny surprise – a nineteenth-century harbour, allegedly Scotland's smallest, carved into the rocks. From this vantage point you will take in stunning views of Tantallon Castle. Despite the castle being in ruin, it is an impressive view.

Access

Seacliff is accessed via a private road from Auldhame farmstead; buses between North Berwick and Dunbar stop just outside here. There is a barrier that opens for a small payment. The track leads down to the beach – keep following it until you reach the car park.

Tyninghame

REGION **East Lothian** LAT/LONG **56.024, -2.594**
GRID REF **NT 630815** BEACH FACES **North-east**
ACTIVITIES **Paddling, walking**

Perfect for a day trip from central Edinburgh, discover a world away from the bustling city at Tyninghame. A wide expanse of golden sand, bordered by tall sand dunes and lapped by rolling waves, this is a truly stunning beach. You can enjoy views out to the mighty Bass Rock, home to a lighthouse and a huge colony of northern gannets, as you take in this special beach.

Access

Buses between North Berwick and Dunbar stop on the A198, two and a half kilometres from the beach. There is a nearby pay-and-display car park a short walk from the beach through a sheltered woodland.

Coldingham Sands Beach

REGION **Scottish Borders** LAT/LONG **55.892, -2.135**
GRID REF **NT 917665** BEACH FACES **East**
ACTIVITIES **Swimming, sailing, surfing, fishing, windsurfing, canoeing**

An idyllic and secluded bay, Coldingham Sands Beach boasts a bumpy headland and striking rock formations scattered along the shoreline. The colourful beach huts lining the top of the dunes make this a picturesque place to spend your day.

The beach is situated within the St Abbs and Eyemouth Voluntary Marine Reserve, and hermit crabs can be seen in the rock pools. Also, thousands of cliff-nesting birds can be spotted at the nearby St Abbs Head Nature Reserve.

Lifeguards patrol this beach on selected days from June to September, and often run a swim safe programme on the beach. During this time dogs must be kept on leads and motors are prohibited in certain areas.

For Marvel fans, head up the road to the nearby fishing village of St Abbs. This was the filming location for New Asgard in *Avengers: Endgame*.

Access

Frequent buses between Berwick-upon-Tweed and St Abbs stop in Coldingham village, just over a kilometre from the beach. There is car parking opposite St Vedas Surf Shop and School. Public toilets (with showers and an accessible toilet) lie at the back of the beach.

Gaelic (Gàidhlig) glossary

Aiseag Ferry
Bàgh Bay
Camas Bay or harbour
Caolas/caolais Narrow, strait/firth
Carraig Rock/fishing rock
Ceann/cinn Headland/point
Claddach/claddaich Shore/stony beach
Cleiteadh Ridge of rocks in the sea

Corran Point of land running into the sea or island seen at low tide
Cuan Sea/ocean
Eilean Island
Loch Lake
Mol Shingle beach
Muir/mara Sea/ocean
Òb/Òbain Little bay

Port Port/harbour
Rubha/rudha Promontory
Sàilean Little inlet
Stalla/stallachan Skerry/rock in sea
Tairbeart Peninsula, crossing/portage
Tràigh Seashore/beach
Uisge Water

The beaches: top tens

Top 10 beaches for natural features

1   Dunaverty Bay, Argyll and Lochaber *p30*
2   Camas nan Geall, Argyll and Lochaber *p41*
3   Fionnphort Bay, Inner Hebrides *p74*
4   Coral Beach, Inner Hebrides *p84*
5   Red Point, the Far North-West *p122*
6   Oldshoremore Beach, the Far North-West *p132*
7   Sandwood Bay, the Far North-West *p133*
8   Cata Sand, the Far North *p152*
9   Sinclair's Bay, East Coast *p159*
10 Cullen, East Coast *p171*

Top 10 beaches for walking

1   Rockcliffe, South-West Coast *p6*
2   Glenan Bay, Argyll and Lochaber *p27*
3   Camasunary Bay, Inner Hebrides *p83*
4   Halaman Bay, Outer Hebrides *p95*
5   Unnamed Beach, Outer Hebrides *p102*
6   Scarista, Outer Hebrides *p107*
7   Sandwood Bay, the Far North-West *p133*
8   Balnakeil Bay, the Far North *p140*
9   Torrisdale Bay, the Far North *p144*
10 Cata Sand and Tresness, the Far North *p152*

Top 10 beaches for running

1   Ayr Beach, South-West Coast *p10*
2   Machrihanish, Argyll and Lochaber *p32*
3   Tralee Bay, Argyll and Lochaber *p37*
4   Crossapol, Inner Hebrides *p63*
5   Unnamed Beach, Outer Hebrides *p102*
6   Seilebost, Outer Hebrides *p108*
7   Sandwood Bay, the Far North-West *p133*
8   Findhorn and Roseisle Beach, East Coast *p167*
9   St Andrews West Sands, East Coast *p175*
10 Tyninghame, East Coast *p180*

Top 10 beaches for cycling

1   Pirnmill, South-West Coast *p14*
2   Ettrick Bay, Argyll and Lochaber *p25*
3   Kilmory, Argyll and Lochaber *p35*
4   Tralee Bay, Argyll and Lochaber *p37*
5   Singing Sands, Argyll and Lochaber *p42*
6   Gott Bay, Inner Hebrides *p64*
7   Scoor Beach, Inner Hebrides *p69*
8   Martyr's Bay, Inner Hebrides *p77*
9   Scarista, Outer Hebrides *p107*
10 Slaggan Bay, the Far North-West *p126*

Top 10 beaches for wild swimming

1   Irvine, South-West Coast *p10*
2   Carradale Bay, Argyll and Lochaber *p29*
3   Ganavan Sands, Argyll and Lochaber *p36*
4   Singing Sands, Argyll and Lochaber *p42*
5   Camusdarach Beach, Argyll and Lochaber *p46*
6   Traigh Shiar, Outer Hebrides *p92*
7   West Beach, Outer Hebrides *p105*
8   Reef, Outer Hebrides *p113*
9   Big Sand, the Far North-West *p125*
10 Portobello, East Coast *p176*

Top 10 beaches for stand-up paddleboarding

1   Ganavan Sands, Argyll and Lochaber *p36*
2   Sanna Bay, Argyll and Lochaber *p41*
3   Traigh, Argyll and Lochaber *p44*
4   Feall Bay, Inner Hebrides *p64*
5   Uisken Beach, Inner Hebrides *p70*
6   Traigh Shiar, Outer Hebrides *p92*
7   Prince's Bay, Outer Hebrides *p101*
8   Baleshare, Outer Hebrides *p102*
9   Big Sand, the Far North-West *p125*
10 Gullane Bents, East Coast *p179*

Index